DAWN SAIL OVER CROOKWOOD

POEMS & POINTELLE

BY

MARK WHELEHAN

FOR SEOS

This book is dedicated to my father, Seos Whelehan, a small selection of whose poems also appear in this book.   He was the son of an Irish politician and maths professor, and was born and brought up in a society in Dublin full of actors, clergy and politicians. He came as a young doctor from Ireland to set up a home in Wiltshire then worked as a Psychiatrist for the National Health Service all of his life.

He was a truly amazing man - engaging, erudite, well read, a deep thinker, a unique character and a very, very kind man. He helped a lot of people, unconditionally, to enjoy their lives and they all love him. Unfortunately, he dedicated his life, with my mother Gertrude, to bringing-up five of us, so was unable to write more.

He did his best to keep a lid on me! I owe him and my mother my life - the family and in turn the friends I have had and have now. I owe to them the ability to attempt all the artistic creation he was unable to achieve.

Cepenpark Publishing Ltd
10 Sandpiper Gardens
Chippenham
SN14 6YH

CepenPark Publishing Ltd

First Published in Great Britain in 2019 by Cepenpark Publishing Ltd
Cover Design by Will Mirehouse & Mimi Kellard
Scanning by Peter King

Mark Whelehan asserts the moral right to be identified
as the author of this work, including all text and images.

A catalogue record of this book
is available from the British Library
ISBN 978 0 9564230 1 6
Printed in Great Britain by

CPI Antony Rowe
Units 1-4 Pegasus Way
Bowerhill Industrial Estate
Melksham, Wiltshire, SN12 6TR

FOREWORD

I awoke early one morning to find myself in my bed sailing over all I surveyed. The land over which I soared, clipping the tree tops, was Crookwood - the Crookwood brook a winding stream below me, eventually the river Wort, a tributary of the mighty Avon. This corner of the Pewsey Vale near Devizes in Wiltshire, where magical things have happened to me, is responsible for inspiring a lot of the last two books and this one - probably a few more as well.

I ploughed on through blue crystal skies witnessing past loves resting, gratefully alone, below in bucolic bliss. Birds nose dived to avoid collision, badgers shot down their holes in fright, deer behind them, foxes, hedgehogs, rabbits, hares. Neighbouring farmers squeaked and growled, staring up in wonderment at my underside - levelling an intended boot no doubt.

When I awoke for a second time I had returned home to my real bed - I think - and I was gazing cross-eyed, out the window. When my sight settled and refocused properly my pet parrot was gabbling a load of nonsense she has picked up from me; my already massive Wolfdane pup was scratching, yawning and stretching to obscure the view. Time to get up and on.

I hear my nephew calling forlornly up the stairwell: *"Uncle Marky - your publisher will be here in a minute!"* I slide, in one lithe movement, from bed to computer and rattle off a hundred or so poems...mumbling: *"That'll do I reckon."*

The rest is history!

MARK WHELEHAN

• • • • • • • • • • • • • • • • •

Other Books by Mark:
Over Crookwood (2016) - Kindle edition
Cassiopeia Lying Eastward (2017) - ISBN 978 0 9564899 5 1

DAWN SAIL OVER CROOKWOOD

In the greater scheme of things
It seems
Nothing really matters
In our dreams...

Springs
A half moon tilted westward
Cocked its head
Orion spread-eagled
Where Betelgeuse bled
Leaned towards the lunar profile
And in some low slung cloud
A serious Dog star barked out loud
Blinked while others winked
A young owl finding his wavering voice
Lonely wailed
While I layed back upon my bed boat and
Gently sailed

Where I went was navigated by that moon
I fled and floated to other worlds festooned
With marvellous and monstrous derring-dos
And overhead Antares' reflecting macaroon
Shone a silver ice beam through an ink lagoon
Arcturus watched me steadily
Glowing like an ember orange-read me

Debating now to jump up and close the scene
The dawn like a capricious lover raced a dark horizon
Exploding highlights across my room
Searchlights for a missing person
Broke joy into a doom and gloom

1

I sat bolt upright from my dream
And crept to the window scene
Outside a cold serene and misty steam
Emanating from the stream of thoughts
The plots and my encounters and my
Repercussive shock
For it was early October
And only five o'clock...

Down over Crookwood brook I float
Though my toes are frozen
Uncoated lay stretched out
My mind bloated with euphoria
My body sleeps
By me I note trees reaching up and scraping underneath
I see my sheep nibbling already on the homefield heath
I hear each tiny working of their tiny teeth

The Tansy like some bossed flying buttress rises out the side
Of a hedgerow architecturally next to vetch
Its flowers like yellow buttons encrusted on its tines letch
Knotty figwort can echo all the sounds from Christmas into spring
I love that name almost more than anything
Wild roses hips like red eyed sleepless pearls in wisps of mists
Perspire their dulled fire
And still I sail on...
While chased by foe a squadron of crow
My sailing boat climbs a little higher so

Once twisted like an endless knot all
My interlinking caused affect now loosens and undoes
Existing in my own karma in love and growing old
Most striking of this scene below is how luminous
Pastilles wash of purple red and aquamarine emitting
Tiny sparks of bugled gold...

As I was passing over the Stroudhill lane
The stream shaken twists in pain
Fountains like whiskey in the jar
A young woman reclines in a woodland glade is counting the beats
As she sings, "In the Cork and Kerry mountains!"
Her name rhymes with Sue
And her finger nails are painted blue
Her hair in Spring sunshine sparkles
Her eyes tattooed
Kaleidoscopic patterns
In wonderment she yawns and stretches
And in ecstasy too
Among a shimmering patch of snowdrops she can touch and see
Which she is
Floating through
Time stops
Fast forwards through seasons
Unforeseeable reasons
This mirror on life is the
The image dancing in her eye's lens
In shades
Autumn and the faces longer
Some pale and wan now
Sad unconsciousness of
Reflections of matter...

Image of floating bed in the pond there
In her mind's eye
My consciousness is the matter
And as the farm ducks waddling
Randomly follow the metaphysical path to it
The spirit of truth swims
Across the water in the black
And whiteness of being
Objective reality displayed in
Their subjective thought

Back to the snowdrops
And daffodils
Winding up my path
In the dark
Only me there...
Quel dommage...
Under a ghostly moon
On my raft
Sailing up a paragraph

DAWN CHORUS

Sun fingers climb windows, touch the ceiling
Creep slowly onwards and invade my room
As they advance, first sounds of life are heard
Distant, hushed, notes of song, faint but clear
Then melodies pure, distinct, with feeling
Swell and surge into a soaring passion
Of full throated music and choral joy
And as the night recedes, light and birdsong
Encompass the fields, woods, garden and lawn
Fill the air and herald the waking day
The cloud clear sky heightens, darkness gone
Now early sounds of rural life resume
As if the world had paused, breathless for the dawn
Still half-asleep in bed I turn and yawn

SEOS WHELEHAN

HER FACE

Face fair; topaz blue eyes shining with grace
Sweet lips that seal her kiss and warm embrace
Gently her wisdom flows, modest and kind
Enriching river of her tranquil mind
Illuminates her life of love and shows
A mirror image of serene repose
Today, dear heart, each time I see your face
You help to exorcise the human race

SEOS WHELEHAN

HER HANDS

Hands slender and small, fingers slim but firm
Joined they raise a manual prayer to heaven
A pleading steeple of faith and hope
Tapering devotion and symmetric grace
Her clasp of handshake genuine and strong
Given with frank pleasure and a smile
She does not miss the empty outstretched palm
But tenderly leaves a gift of kindness
Her sadness when we part, with hands half raised
Waving farewell, and stemming welling tears
All vanishes in welcoming embrace
Enchanting me, imprisoned by those hands
Whose loving touch can calm a childish rage
And give a gentle blessing to my soul

SEOS WHELEHAN

G

I die each time I leave you, and you cry
When I return we're born again in love
Merging the flowing cross-tides of our lives
Within whose mingling waters we're complete
Whilst holding me in glowing grace and joy
Your heart being fire rapt by our loving flame
Knows; that though I leave you for the last time
I shall return, quietly, by night
Lying so close but light upon your bed
Then you; half-waking, as I breathe your name
Will softly sigh, and smiling, reach for me
Knowing, I'm always with you, like our love
An eternal star, shining forever
And you my soul, need never cry again

SEOS WHELEHAN

THE DARK LAKE

Day fades slowly, shadows deepen
Dim twilight shades a dusky world
Mists merge, drift and shroud the evening
Now pitter-patter sounds of rain
Surge to a more collective drone
Soak'd trees huddle in the downpour
Darkness advances, embracing
The lakes fringes and the waters edge
One no longer sees the shape nor form
The night sky and the stars have gone
Always the rain comes on and on
This is a wet and lonely place
We lie here, part of the cold earth
We are the night waiting for dawn

SEOS WHELEHAN

THE SILVER MARTYR

A wooded vale with sunlight and green shades
Tree covered slopes rise steeply skywards
Maundrells lake curves with undulating verges
And brimming shallows fringed with dipping boughs
A grassy mound surveys the southern end
And northwards welcomes its life giving stream
A child of Wiltshire downs and rivulets
Stealing secretly from a leafy hide
Into the calm smooth surface of the lake
Ruffl'd only, by foamy wakes of scurry'ng coots
Proprietary swans cruise serenely
Unperturbed, aloof, and dignified
Spellbound, I spend hours casting and casting
Then hold the silver martyr in my hand

SEOS WHELEHAN

A FIGMENT MY MUSE

I never really really knew really
From that day I drew that to this merely
That that picture that has rested in my head
Was anything more than a spirit of you
Lying on your bed

Which leads me constantly wondering
Which was first to arrive the thought of you
Or the inner drive
The need to conjure up an image
Of you nursing your lovely head on a naked bed
Save for a pillow

Those unrested nights
Your mind never clicking off
You texted me and I replied
I took the opportunity for you to muse
My rhymes and give your view to
So late until we both felt so dead tired
We fell asleep at separate times
With waiting messages to reply to

So on it went soon to get up
Looking forward to something now
And so it went on for weeks and months
A year or two
A virtual relationship never given up
Nothing grave nothing strained
That blossomed and it grew
Without us hardly meeting in the flesh

The odd chanced rendezvous
Beside the Crookwood brook
The closest we ever came to...
Your bare neck and hair like sunshine
Soft cajoling voice teasing reprimanding
And those nervous tired eyes demanding warmth
But always shining green and live
Driving me insane
The pain and the time just flew
It would never be the same after
Though

And then down came the rain
I smelt your breath on the inner vein
Ourselves no further apart melted closer
Than the thickness of a window pane
But both of us knew we drew closer
Too inside a hide we'd built
With an inner view
At Markie's bar the gin imbibed
Rather more than few proscribed

For no reason just randomly
The black plastic buckets falling reckless
Empty tossed 'bout by winds
Kept to catch the rain
Tipped at such an angle coincidentally I feel
As delivering some canned refrain though real
Or interstellar sign Jodrell banked the view

Somedays clouds could hardly move
Koala shapes huffed and puffed
But sat exhaustedly
In this corner of a cobalt sky
Underneath Crookwood the lamb
Under the larch tree
Stirred the grass green heard never a word
This mead and spouted leat
Like a billiard baize beneath our feet

So snipped by Soay and Jacob's teeth
No longer than the bright green fuzz
Some pubescent haze bearded the curved twigs
This our tiny flock under insects hover buzz
Sipped from the water trough paled in the sun
Bleated hard and long there was
A message in their mournful song
Glowing planets collided sparking above
There in the Ham orchard
Over Crookwood

Those nights of stars and moons
And minds ballooning into a silver lunar pool
Your nocturnal thoughts collected sumped
Spooning spinning cocooning like a metal floss
Their reconnoitre round and round your favourite
Swirling heavenly bodies
Galactic trips drip through your mind
Like a tap not tightened-leaks
And over time was caught empty and void
And on my sweat blown steed I rushed and blushed
To save you hushed and mopped
Your fettered brow

Never let it be said our mothers bred gibbers
Sending shivers me hearties down our spines
All hands on deck and above board
Out of this bosom of land known as Crookwood
There came a cry "Ahoy There!" Espy!
Fashioned from it wooden shanks
A sculpted trophied form
Which sailed forth on taught ropes
Snapping sails our galleon
Stormed the staring glaring deriding ranks
Performed she heaved and spanked
Tossed and ploughed a mighty furrow
Punched bellow the belt of the salt kissed waves

Our profanities proclaimed and peppered
Through sapphire skies
And late at night that mighty black leopard leapt
No beings awaken to fright
And left its eye as the moon
Marooned a yellow macaroon
Oak and elm wood long broken boiled
Into small colonies of trees was rolling
In an emerald green wake of serpentine
Stirred the spring seasons
Herbs sprinkled on a stew

Something magical a catalytic brew bubbled and rose
The lip spilled out over everywhere and nowhere
In the air a lonely swallow flew an omen
Like 'n albatross sailing through brought early hope

While under the moss iced
Clandestine chapstone lid
Hid dead in his cist and cool as flint
A stone age man
Yet no one knew he did

And that was when your saddened heart was vulnerable
Yet great dreams fought back in and in the end bought out
The black hole pulling through your soul
A yearning deep in your womb
Of a mind to grow foetus-like
Not a shadow of unkindness thought
No doubt lingers or fingers finds to point
Paying for other peoples sins
So ordered is your maternal process
It was only when you laid awake at nights ends
Your conscience gnawed and grinded
We both were blinded
But all I knew and I almost blew it
Was that I just couldn't share you

Both of us reckoned there was a love
And I cannot draw that
But both of us knew there was a synergy too
And I cannot flaw that
That it was simple and amazing
And a lovely pure feeling
An' that that was True
Our last message coming through
Also coming true

For what ever else I tried to do
At least I let you be you.
You told me so
And you let me create - words and things
And a lovely pure feeling free of sin
Shining through
And that was love
And it was deep
And that was truth infused
And all that was because of you
My muse.

BESIDE THE BROOK STARLIGHT SHONE

I sat down beside the brook
To gaze up at the stars and looked there for some sign
Because someone had my love forsook
And I could not shake it from my mind

Yet in the bleary light of dawn that now crept across my view
I couldn't understand nor could I take it
Though many times I'd taken love for granted
I raved and ranted and loudly swore
That you should have rejected mine

The sun like a blister broke and pain from light made me choke
On unrequited passion
That such a thing could happen to poor me wasn't rational...

As mist clung to the babbling stream racing like a live thing
I drew my fingers through the green sand and sketched your face
The gleam of sun turned colours like a rainbow within the steam
Which shrouded my thoughts like a sullen cloak
Then I cried out loud that such beauty
Could enter my troubled mind
The sun appeared through the cloud
As if an orange rind cured
And while this weird dawn broke wide
Like marmalade pouring cross the fields
A shadow of a form appeared
And in my minds eye I feared nothing from
I stood as if I woke
And from a dream had broken free
And raced across the sodden fields of dew
And I was singing as I sped but never did I reach the other side
An arm outstretched and bid me bide my time
So I sat down

16

Yet I looked about and still I sat beside the stream
Where earlier I had seen your face and traced a pattern in the sand
The stars fast and sure and true still shone down on me
And in that sort of gloam the starlight shone
I upped and wandered home...

BLANK CANVAS

I was swimming in this pool of glory
When someone unearthed this story
Along the lines of past loves
Swings the long train of past love I write...
I'd been clothed in lotion
Consumed by some soft notion
That in all this idyll
Nature was predictable

Across the flooding fields worm stuffed crows
Ejaculate contented croaks
And as I lift to drain the pale
Sated standin' in a rill
Drifts the haunting wail
Of a goods train exhausted shunting up
The vale onto a rising hill

Inches slowly like a sleepy grass snake
Its sombre vibrations shake
Dew from off the nodding daffodil
And in some dark tunnel
Searching dithering mice to kill
The spray sparks along the track
Their platinum bordering ranks
Trails of smoke rise up until
It mingles with the low hung mist
Dissipating as the sun burst rays of
Brilliance spill

I want to start all over again again

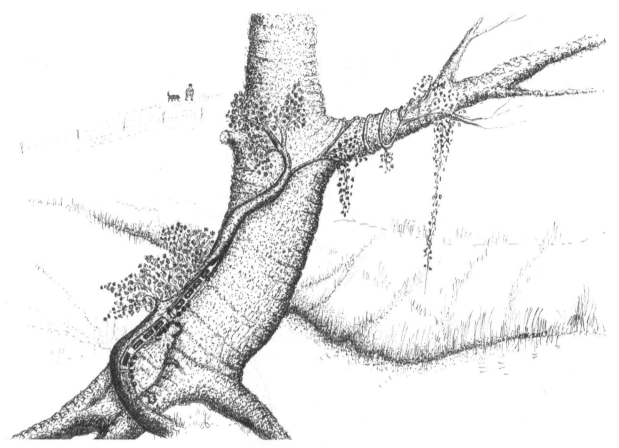

Oh I dunno
I want a lot of white paint
Spread on that canvas though
I switch on a light in a darkened room
Suddenly an almighty boom
Am doing a landscape of a canvas
I need to catch all the light
That ever was
On a stretched cotton
Six by four

19

The world is flat now
We are no more and in
That whiteness
Someone opens a tiny door
And in steps Adam
Climbs a tree plucks an apple
Throws to Eve
They close the door and then conceive
The pictures painted for ever now

I stoop and find an apple
Survivor of the frosts as I
Bite into it juices run down my chin
A voice within
Wrong time wrong place toooo old
To taste me
You shoud've left me
Don't waste me

The splashing of the stream so bare
The trees in spring
I sit so near its everywhere
And everything
Just water and light

A white horse burst through and onto the blank space
The fluidity of wild motion
No commotion or clicking of gears
Instinctive change of mode and pace
In synergy with time and grace

As I Sit Quietly Talking With You

I had a dream the other night
My head held tightly in a vice
And all the things and all the people
I had ever known
Were mixed up altogether in a primordial fight
Careering down a watershoot
My life is racing on
And all are falling over me
As I sit on the phone
Quietly talking with you

I wave at them to keep the noise down
But they carry on
Tumbling and falling shouting brawling
What a carry on
I draw the curtains dowse the lights
But ... they crawl small back in my head
And shout

And all are falling over me
As I sit on the phone
Quietly talking with you

21

THE LADY OF BLUEBELL WOOD

Like cave drawings inside out
These gnarled roots and trees
Had figures I could see
Within their frieze
Something sombre shout
To me a narrative
And as the sun shines on
The fall out of years ago
Old tongues conspire
And talk in whispers still
Of what it's all about

I'm on my own it's very early
There's no one else out
So I start about my
Thoughts of what these
Rough hieroglyphs
Tell me in their story
Of chivalry and knight
Errants in
An' all their glory

Whether I awoke this soul
Or because so lost
In hearing my own voice
I awoke as well
Suddenly from nowhere
A girl with bright red hair
Materialises in the morning air
Walks in and out the long
Grasses with her loyal dog

But on closer scrutiny we see
That she is quite old really
But dressed the same
She ever was
Oblivious of passing time
And what it does

She sings all the time
She leaps over
The tangled roots and
Into that secret wood
Wherein forever blue
Bell blankets grew
And roe deer lay and
Over centuries rabbits
And badgers great mounds
Have built amongst that blue-
Turquoise quilt they say

Still the smell of ash
Smoke hint-pervades
The suffocating scented bells
And as your feet stir the tilth
Black charcoal twigs remain where
Wild flowers now invade
In the centre of the wood
A massive black trunk is lain
And as the sun spokes stalk
Through the canopy above
Particles of dust suspended
Within the drunken air wreathe

Settle black as soot ...
and if
You grasp a frond you wear a glove
Falls upon your hair and arms
And in the air you breathe
I would have sworn fain
In the centre of this wood
This stricken fallen giant tree
Takes the form of some huge
Horned dinosaur once slain

I see the lady approach the
Mighty trunk and kneel
And gently stroke its
Head and feel it fondly
I am dumbstruck as
To what to do or say
So with the hairs
Arisen on my neck
I back quietly away

Nearby the local Inn
So welcoming
Is fondly named
The Saint George
And over a pint I enquire
Purposely off hand
About a woman
With red hair who
I had earlier seen
So suddenly there

In shock when they recover
From what I've spoken
This story unearths itself from old
Dreams I have broken
The wife of a once local Lord
George Pendragon
Of the manor
Who some say took a lover
When she feared
He wouldn't return alive
From fighting overseas

The lord wounded from war and love
When he discovered on his return
And heard the word she'd taken
A lover in his absence so shaken
Tracked him down and brought
Him to this place and
After dispatching him
Set fire to him as well
But in so doing spilled
Some liquid fuel upon himself
So accidently perished
Himself in flames within
That same bluebell wood

That his wife a fiery redhead
So possessed ran off
Afeared them both slain
Has never come back
Or ever been seen again

CHIFF CHAFF

I hear it even when I am not there
Down that corridor my head spins
Like a Bacon painting smudged blur
Through an avenue of trees and bushes
There when the lights thin
Its grating lisp when I was younger pushed along
It shared my blushes tumbled in the long grass

This bird distinct where nothing else cried out
Kept up a beat that evocates it all
Cricket balls shoot across
Like cannons plunder on the plain
Flat tanks creeping never gain
White mad figures dive, they shred on the tarmac drive
Still no more emotion in that steadfast call though in its tiny eye
It must've seen the fall
My new shoes barely reach the ground
Everything in that daunting glazed hall sounds
Still in my earlike shell when it explodes
I hear only that diminutive thing calling

A masquerading great tit does its best repetitive
Instead but not so bold and loud in tone'n colour
This quiet chapter though dog-eared's
More subtle's better read

Rock like cake thunder speeches thumping tables
Impact terms in lakes of tea
It hops from stem to twig camouflaged immaculate
Not much larger than a bee
Mopped up with bread and library sat in
Staring out the window over reference books in Latin

24

Ricocheting out across the leas "Let me go please!?"
Nod cows the crowd applause and echo down past's closed doors
Laws of the thicket now emerge pushed about from room to room
Chiff chaff chiff chaff chiff chaff chiff chaff breaks the gloom

It sews a link-paid continuity to the rolling film spool in my
Private shed of Soay sheep spring a 'leaping it accompanies them in
A Choreographed play on an otherwise cold April day
Swept clean with an old broom, after hiding in doors open on it sped
Only the wisp of laboratory gas and acid terror bites its bitten heels
And ass like a tiny train on relentless it chuffs along its secret way
Incognito unnoticed in the heaving crowd yet it's voice so very loud
Please let me paint it a mighty rainbow shroud this tiny bird so beige so grey

Exquisite in its tempus fugitive its seems to live so long
Where one falls another lifts the baton and the same song rages on
And like a warble fly it burrows neath the skin
Comes out the other side still chiff-chaffing
Yet in the autumn it goes and with it goes its call
As with the wind the leaves crisp brown and fall
Blow out in winters mall

We've learned of life its slow molasses creep the cold underpasses
And the masses show the sores of losing time there is no time
You Are an individual a man.
But hardly am still stuck in time
And none left to be

Still that call of the chiffchaff enters into me
There when I wake in my spinning bed
Like a sweet tinnitus a broken record faltering
And there long may it continue till
Like that summer 's call at autumns fall
My winter comes all's dead

25

CROOKWOOD BROOK

Many times dressed for time too late
Gone down to that stream meandering
Across the fields from the railway line
Through that rusty hinged gate
Openings to a wider world
My heart was heavy
My loves esteem needed to
Redeem humming a verse
From a nursery rhyme

Racing along that Folly track
Escaping raw memories of a recent spat
Stars shone Moon smiled down
Reflected benignly
Aldeboran Arcturus Betelgeuse and Pleidaies too
Played with my opened soul
A levy to their beauty true- my faith in them
Forever being there

My mind inside a black hole
Entered in so deep and cured my sins
Stole my troubles for dilution
Which I poured into that brook as
Gazing into its racing depth
Seemed to draw my worries from me
Flew away to sea
And solved the problems
My heart and dreams ablution

Owls hoot checked to hear and digest
Paced on cracking twigs and crackling leaves
Released a dry sardonic compacted history
Mouse lives in a pellet
Teeth bones and velvet
Bounced a bundled message
At my feet upon the ground

Distant train transporting sounds
Echoed long journeys through my head
And out the other side
Shuttled off ...and died

Unsettled pigeon down
Fell soft as snow to earth
Kissed it brushed my face
Gazing up at so near so far
The winking blinking electric
Universe of endless countless stars

Babbling waters twinkling in their light
As down a bank I slide
Planets circling to prelate a coming alignment
Replace my sadness with delight
Reflect back to me such joy
Washing like a salve
Absolves

BUTTERCUPS IN PINK

Buttercups buttercups
As far as the eye can see
Butter'd up butter cut spread
Even as a mental picture
Come sweeping up to me
Underneath your chin
Shakes Golden bling
Life's just a little film we're in
Flash backs to me of things
Caught in an early Spring

Endless frosted fields with udders tapped
Glow forcing the shadow's shrink
The sun comes up and
Underneath the trees
Drips form to drink
With chestnut leaves as large as plates
And panticles inverted icicles
Hawthorn hedges icing'd
Off into infinities

Yellow green and white hues
Where black and white
Cows swim under the azure blue
The only colours here construed
Cascading over a brink

There whether or not I think of them
Confusion of love with possession of
Will never be woven with serenity
Race out until the milky way
And off into outer space

Yellow brushstrokes wash and gild
A carpet rania glides out beyond
Sunlight by a painter seen
A million goblets in between
Drunk on dew with Oberon 'n Titania's
Waving wand

Crescendo'd silver lark climbs trilling
Tongue is lost as chilling sun's set
Redness sends a shroud
And as the ghostly moon ascends
Frees ebb and flow of waves amend
The yellow goes and dies
Across these fecund pastures rolling
Comes up and down
And in bluffs rise and sink

So Artemis lunar waking
Discovers from her prison breaking
Her searching platinum rays division
Create an alien prism where she sees
Across my fields aligned
Those silhouetted buttercups
In pink

DEEP AN' CRISP AN' EVEN

Through the split of velvet curtain
Shot the sun from frosted lands
Shards of splintered light across
Revealed to her old aged hands
Black holes from footsteps
On the snowfield trudged
The old man's figure

Growing smaller out of sight
She stole reminisces of
Saint Wenceslas and Snow White
The carol lingered on her lips
The cold breath froze her finger tips
So near the window blew a kiss
This virtual white antithesis
To her heavy soul

Uma Uma Uma Talthida Talthida Muscida
Tav Upsilon Theta Talthida Talthida Muscida
The Great bear is coming...

As the robin hovered catching
Early midges' virgin flight
A glimpse of something in the window
Triggered dropped the fly with fright ...
Marmalade moments of
This sunny day unrolled
Spilled out like a new paint
Across the countryside
Rare day ran red into a raw night
Roared a borealis scorched the
Homeward birds in roosting flight

Sat a cup of steaming coffee drained
Mulled at thoughts strained her eyes
And chewed slowly on some toast
Like it was some
Church taken communion host
That old guy had gone walkabout...
Walkabout again she mused
He was such an interesting chap
To talk to she enthused
Indeed has panglossian extreme optimism
Chutzpah modus operandi
And again once more she rused

Nibbled- miles away-at a cracked open
Hazel nut careful not to bite some shell
Most of the time his brain was making
Decisions telling without him being - well -
Consciously aware!
Our consciousness summoned up
To hear see or smell
To decide if a sudden situation
Needs dispel forsooth a threat
Or opportunity negates avoiding punity
Once before given him hell
After cracking a tooth

He found an apple on the floor
He bit into and ate it more
Like chomping on a lollipop
So frozen to the core
Electric shock of pain was born

But in a state of aspic caught
The nerve inside his tooth was torn
Yet nothing in his brain was scored
He sank into a reverie
And drank the aspect in
Smooooooth like gin

Perched on a stile a'while
The 'currant bun' warmed his booth
Weltered whoreson woodcock split
Spatchcocked spit-cooked spilt he
Sweltered in the Beltane sun
He marvelled at the random
Wanderings of wood tunnelling worms
Minutely etched where
It'd turned and squirmed
A full stop and a detour where it met a knot
The tiny insect left hieroglyphic codes for what
Newts and toads hibernated nearby in iris tubers
Like an Egyptian plinth showed forbears fought
On the handrail of his footbridge
Newly spanning the boiling flooding
Ever spoiling capricious River Wort
Where Crookwood brook
A tributary spurts

Enterin' a 'Flow State'
He scratched his balding pate
Purple Portugal purpurite intuitive
His heightened mento-physical rate
Shot with minerals in the water's spate
He was totally immersed in activity

Without rational thought
His conscious awareness dulled
Fought hidden parts of his brain
Took over dispelling fear
While swirling down a drain

As he dried down his preponderances
He sat on a stump nestled on his rump
And felt like a new man scratched his pole
Purple Portugal purpurite-intuitive furtive
Refreshed in body and soul - spiky looked
Next t'a bored out water hole
Within this Crookwood brook
The greensward beyond the bank
Shouldered through the freeze
In golden rays smouldered
Where rising arrows chocolate faced
Pochard joined a 'V' of geese

Her face in a cloud of sparks shot
Skywards too and
Exploded on his mental eye
Though dissolving gentle as a lullaby
He now hummed
Uma Uma Uma Talthida Talthida Muscida
Like trees fall subside into the
Water after floods gum opened
Brought the sap like dripping plum
Down the roots held on like ropes
No hope the arboretum bloodbled
Swept away and out to sea

33

This was a magical matinee
That flickered in his head
Waves thrashed giant seaweed pods
Which had given up their dead
Gods unleashed on far off worlds
Flew high above his head
Were fighting beyond this azure blue
And on Orion's shoulder slew
Maybe moored up aliens fed
And bled with awful wounds
As they breast fed their babies too

What did everything mean it seemed
Bringing children onto this planet
Alcoholic husbands leaving mums behind
Escaping nights out on their own
Sat back with some old ancient reticent
Sphinx-like purring cat to help their minds...

First stars blinked open on a wide blue plain
He started on a song deep outside his brain

"I had this vision I suppose
For purpose to transpose
Some words into a song along
Where angel's kiss conspires to miss
Where my bucolic youth has gone

A vision of a sword that hung
Down from Orion's belt
So young and strong it shines
He his mettle never melts
He brandishes it reaps and cuts
At shadows of a love he's lost

34

Yet I too like him has sores
Which as I hurt ravishes his heart
From a maiden in distress
Who bid me aid her gentleness
Now ignores her knight the work I've done
She blessed steps back in the darkness
So egoless

Whose fading image once
Furnaced like exploding coals
Which smote now smoke out
As reticent fires about me die
He though still confounds
All odds as in some rage
Hurls meteors at gods which often
Fall down upon this little Earthen sod
And below we opened- mouthed gaze up
As descending gold dust swirls
Reflect with awe what's going on
Light-years from our world

He had a heart that wept not
But as the day approaches near
His chivalry accords
That as the night recedes
The mighty hunter falls
Upon his fading sword"

The late amber moments of this winter's day
Folded up like a rolled up newspaper
Of life's tapestry now
Inexorably read into another night of ink

The steeple punctured a perfect swirl
A cloud curl that sat like a blur of cream
Inside a sky of raspberry
The stream flowed purple to the sea
The evening sunset subsided dripped
Over the Ham orchard
A hound cried a fox stirred heard
An owl scream turned round went back to sleep
A badger looked over its
Greying shoulder sniffed the cold air a day older
Before descending down
Into its warm pungent musty cette

Aquamarine to violet- damson- black morphed the sky

A shooting star gliding by
Described a perfect
Arc over a chimney stack
Unaware below three ladies in
Amongst the homemade bakes
At the farm shop stow gossiping
When one who's shopping sniffled tearful aches
At her recently departed Jack
Three miles as the crow flies
Behind the Market town church
Three hooded youths were discussing
How cool it was shooting crack

Across the cosmos a yearly re-enactment
Three kings on camels chase a star
With rank intent and mirth
That brings about the birth
Of the greatest religious acrobat

In lakeland fells Sunday bells
And ancient yarns
Drift down and echo
Muffled in murky mountain tarns
What's it all about he thought
As he fought to undo
The staying clinking chains rattling like a plate

He heard a quote in distant tongues relate
'The business of life
Is the acquisition of memories
In the end that's all you have'

A breeze gently swayed the hazel staves
As if to stay the racing cloud
The face of the present clings
But is time just relative
And not important in
The greater scheme of things
He thought...

Where are the hearts
I once wore on my sleeve
Where are the souls of soldiers
Fought and bent on battlefields
..He looked up at the sky weep
Where behind a cloud the moon sleeps
He could not see the woods for the trees spoke
And whispers in their shadows made
The hairs on his back creep

...Encrusted diamonds almost
Froze his hand onto the gate
He hurriedly undid the chains
Jingled loose tunes
It swung open like a rune's
Pathway to another place
Constellations' tinkled stars winked
Showerlike lamps in pattern order
Shining landing lights on another plane

Moss covered lichen-studded
Arms stretched out like
Oak trees looking up and asking
At these wondrous heavenly bodies basking
Am I going insane

He trundled on like an elephant careering
Trumpetin' new lyrics to an ole song
"Semantics swirling bound inside an old and used newspaper cap!"
Great gulp of icy air
"Flushed the gargling vicar leaps in lady's knickers into a giant gin trap!"
Down the crunching white snow-blossomed lane
Bedecked be buggered - he swayed cavorting

Gazing up again Cassiopeia like a massive
Doubled 'You'
Dreamed reclining beauty vane awry
And snooty too gave the eye blue
Tempting Orion feted to admire her by
Lying eastward dying on his
Brilliant unbuckled sword of burning gold
In this winter's sky so black
Like an adders eye so cold
He was beckoned back by some word a cry
Fangs and teeth like barbed wire
Tore into his shins and thighs
Yet he staggered onwards blinded...

Back at her darkened window
Lit only by the snow she cried
looked down at her aging hands
Something wild suave and earthy
She felt about this guy...

39

Nothing behind to stop his fall
As he bent backwards 'neath
Taking in this vastness with all
His naked eye Triangulum
High above hovered in a sheath
Like a stealth crafted warring dove
Pleiades and Ursa minor
Waltzing round Polaris shoved
Maia Electra Alcyone fought Hyades
With bare knuckle fisted hands

Struck up below in tribute ghosts
Look up from some small brass band
On a deserted village stand ephemeral strains-
Fades away on the Midnight breeze
Kochab and Ferak's watery lights
Freeze before stalking submarines
All blended to the snorting Taurus
With testosterone for genes
Where all their heavy magnetic elements
Try to halt the bull
Aldeboran keeps his distance still
And how he shines apart from
Deltas Thetas Sigmus though they tug and pull

...Alkaid Mizar Alioth Megrez Phecda
Al Kaphrah Uma Tania Tania
Merak Dubhe Tav Upsilon Theta
Talthida Talthida Muscida
The vanguard and great bulk of
Bear casts its awesome shadow there where

Drunken sailors chipper singing shanties by Big Dipper
Too late their clipper run aground where
Soon they're lost and scuppered cursing fete
Sound like Russians pointing up
To sounds cocooned ducking heads
To concentric orbits of their moons

Megrez Phecda behind drive the ursine thighs
Merak and Dubhe navigate the bear
Declaring truly north too tardy for these mariners
Who like boobies swear bailing out they shout at
Tav Upsilon and Theta who sweat and fret there
While Muscida the Great bears nose
Sniffs them out with its snout and
Hails Alkaid Mizar Alioth
Three Arabian daughters of the bier
Their work cut out swish its tale
While bringing up the rear

Maybe so great the grizzly mass of bear
Sent gravity waves everywhere
And so they sprung from outer space
Out to Earths tiny face pushing
Causing pressure there

Breathing heavily
And gaining his balance from a swoon
A light broke the horizon
As from a dying concave moon
Reflections darting from a silver spoon
Dawn came as a shock he
Stumbled home at a rush

Though lost in semi darkness
He'd gained a track
Of black and hawthorn bush
Where started up a dawn chorus
Led by a solo from an operatic thrush

Remembering her fair head in amongst
The sparks- impetuosity ferocity
Pouring out like a human Roman candle
Lit at both ends too hot to handle
She shook with temper when she
Wouldn't get her way with men
Though not a religious girl her
Humanity was riddled with profanity then
She believed herself above and
Beyond discretion and respect
A belligerent pocket rocket tesseract

...As he veered into a bend
Blood red berries soft as cherries
Bounce apart and send themselves
A wave into a bush off kilter
Other gravity waves push him
On collision course a force
Fell from heaven to glut the blight
Offering the hungry fauna a variety
A spice of life

Suddenly the old man touched his chest
And felt pain running down his arm
He thrust his other now bent double
To save himself from doing harm
It was as if a great and grizzly bear hugged him
And was squeezing out his last breath

As he fell into a thicket
Chased by an Ursine death
Exploded frosted smoking ice
Shook the bushes in this wildness
Nothing else moved and no one spoke
All his past and present came
And blended into all he was
For this old bloke

Simply a human occurrence
Least relevant to animal folk
Thank God Thank god I'm going like this
Thank you god he gasped at last he choked
At last!

A wind blew final blighted moment
The night departed dawn broke
Everywhere was very whited

A pair of glorious hawfinches alighted
On branches encrusted with diamonds
Greedily feasting this repast
On fallen rose hips from the blast
Began their familiar rasping call

Winters spell again was cast

DO NOT BE DISMAYED 1

I ran up the track beside a stream
Trying to run a way from
My head which chased after me
We both fell together into a spate
Of water rushing to the sea
And there I entered a wet dream
Laying flat on the river 's bed

Thoughts like trees full laden bent
I saw them through the fundament
Fears like badgers foxes hares came
And audienced my loud refrain unaware
For all they heard was mumbled words
Absurd drowning raving song
To which they did not belong

I tried to clear my heart's lament
But the brook held me in its arms
And out beyond in new cut fields
A bird flew cooing like a dove
But as it soared it turned to talk
It introduced itself a hawk

Hovering over it surveyed
And called to me don't be dismayed
And came back down two earth and laid
A single golden egg

Something forced me up and out
As I recouped upon the bank
An apple lay down by my side

I ate it feverishly white I tried to think

But water emptied from my soul
I tried to re construct that dream
But out behind the arboreal curtain
The moon rose splendid framed by steam
Of early morning mists

And I had become a wisp of air
With all around carpeted in light and sound
And your golden hair swept past me swirled
But I had no hold on it
Like a grasping spirit from another world
And floated like great cresses in
That stream that had become
Wider than the river Nile

And your cherubic smile
Broke wider than the dawn
Which raced to chase the moon away
And gave way to the settling sun
Over and over and over again for ever
This repeated like my souls refrain

For once I laid eyes on your form
I have never really been forlorn
And never have I doubted it
Before
Except when I lay down and mused
And tempted myself with negative scenarios

And so embracing your smile
I too lay down a while
Which lasted forever uptil now
And heard again from up above that
Message from that metamorphosed dove
Do not be dismayed

Do Not be Dismayed 2

I ran up the track beside a stream
Trying to run a way from
My head which chased after me
We both slipped and somehow
Fell together into a spate
Some where next to an opened gate
Of water rushing to the sea
And there I entered a wet dream
Laying flat on the river 's bed

Thoughts like trees full laden bent
I saw them through the fundament
Fears personified in badgers foxes rabbits
Came and audienced my loud refrain
But all they heard was mumbled words
An absurd drowning raving song
To which they did not belong

I tried to clear my hearts lament
But the brook held me in its arms
And out beyond in new cut fields
All the creatures ran dispersed
Agoraphobically

45

A horse ran changed into a cow
They raced a cross across a meadow
I swept a hand across my forehead
And I swam in a bubble burst epiphany
And from somewhere in the air withheld
Down where I sank
In watery shadows there began
A waft of blossom from the past

It lasted and I glimpsed reflections
Briefly in the surface skin
Of my own face blood-drained
And thin

That scent I know so welled within
And in a tremor
You washed over me
And you watched over me

And I was saved just then
When all the while
Wild birdsong twined
From a warbler echoed in and columbined
Along the dull depths as down a tunnel
In my mind

The cross changed to a bow
And wondrous colours
Became prayers shot about
Like multicoloured arrows
Shared by a multitude
Dipping humans in the river which
Had been my little brook

Something slithered neath my feet
Became a train which hooted as it moaned
A lonely capsule bearing many familiar
Waving faces racing underground
All clasping one small book
A bird flew cooing like a dove
But as it soared it turned to talk
It introduced itself a hawk

Hovering over it surveyed
And called to me
"The world may not be what it seems."
"Do not be dismayed!"
And came back down to earth and laid
A single golden egg

Something forced me up and out
As I recouped upon the bank
An apple lay down by my side
I ate it feverishly while I tried to think
I sank I must be on the brink of shrinks
With the view to entering a
Black hole and breaking in through
An event horizon's film and skin
And maybe down a wormhole tide
I'm pulled out the other side

As water emptied from my soul
I tried to re-construct that theme
But out behind the arboreal curtain
The moon rose splendid framed by steam
Of nightmares' early morning mists
And drew me back into its dream

I had become a wisp of air
With all around carpeted in light and sound
And your golden hair swept past me swirled
But I had no hold on it
Like a grasping spirit from another world
And floated like great cresses in
That steam that had become
Wider than the Nile

And your everlasting smile
Broke wider than the dawn
Which raced to chase the moon away
And gave way to the settling sun
Over and over and over again for ever
This repeated like my souls refrain

But something shook me violently
I came round sudden with a start
An old man stood over me
Who nearby kept hives of bees
Covered from head to toe in these

"Have you been stung!?" he asked me
His face so serious concernedly
I think he knew more than he said
I smiled and replied "No! I'm ok"
Like that new day
Which around us grew

For once I laid eyes upon your form
I have never really been forlorn
Or sworn allegiance to another
And never have I doubted it
Before
Except when I daydreamed and mused
And tempted myself with negative scenarios
And so embracing your smile my love
I too lay down a while
Which lasted forever uptil now
And heard again from up above that
Message from that metamorphosed dove
Do not be dismayed!

EMMA

Rang the doorbell next the
Chimes and old blue painted car tyre
With forget me nots hanging down
And tumbling thyme
The only bright surprise oasis
In that decaying mundane town

And you appeared wearing
A string of autumn leaves you
Wreathed along the road trees into a crown
That serious moment in your eyes
And sad enigmatic frown
Which broke into a dawn awakening smile

Where in your under down you danced
Like swaddling clothes you led me round and
Round and coiled me on a sliver wire
And in that dingly dell I fell from
Tiny fingers on your maiden hand

It's true it's true all you said
Inside your head all that thought read
My cynical eaten mind was fought and beaten
You had knowledge far beyond
The confines of that giddy frame
Like a precocious pixie with a wizards brain

Where does she get it from
I thought my silence held
You told me things
I'd never gained in so short a time
But you had formed opinions well
Articulate so erudite and argued

Tell me again of your dreams
Racing round the room inside my head
Littered cushions half eaten bread
The streams of tears the ring of laughter
At the random rubbish I had said

Still ringing now as I muse back
You told of how your younger brother strode
In and cleared the flat of booze
To save you from your self
Worried you'd be left upon the shelf

And cakes to eat from your birthday spread
And in that Buddha pose you sat
Not an inch of fat but like a sunstruck butterfly alit
Like a photograph developed reflected on the
Lenses of my aging eyes

Tinkling like a sprinkling of goldfinch
On a welcome tongue you rose crescendo'd
Your eyes snapped like their folding wings shut
Alighted on your silent lidded lips then
Collapsed a final fling and flew through the azure air
Descended acquiesced all done

Your perfect form arose-had risen from the clay
It no way did you justice but just this
Sat me exhausted and exhilarated on the
Very tip of that ravelled
Storm tossed bed
And listened to you thinking out aloud

A waterfall of newly formed ideas
Poured into my head you leapt up and off
I left you to your chores
Wakened from the dead

FANTASY 1 - THE VENUS FLY TRAP

I walked around the churchyard dazed
The sun was hazy and it didn't
Feel the same place in the day
I was trying to workout anyway
How we came to run and shout
But no one heard
Or cared about
The night before

When I asked you for a gin
I never thought this would begin
I wonder now how it never ended

Somehow you said this leads to sin
And gazing at the stars you prophesied
That Mars and Venus
Would always come between us
If we ever lied or pretended

The lights came on the stars went out
In the houses every time
We screamed and shouted
Then all subsided as we sat in awe of
That throbbing cosmos all about

Sitting there upon the hill
We saw the milky way lay still
Stretching out across the sky
Why oh why oh why oh why
Did we never hold each other's kiss

And in the blinking of an eye
The moon switched off and waved goodbye
And everything that ever was
Was out there beyond us
Passing by

The galaxies turned on their sides
And Cassiopeia like a swan flew off
And all along the streetlamps shone
Like a runway for Cygnus the Swan to land
You stretched your arms and gave a cry
I saw the twinkling in your eyes
I caught you falling backwards
And she landed in your hand

On us and on the ghostly trees
In Potterne churchyard on our knees
The frost was crawling
But we didn't care
We sang a chorus as just before us
You pointed out across the vale
A shooting star broke up and paled
Just above our nearest sun
Alpha Centauri

FANTASY 2 - A MESSAGE ON THE WIND

...We blew a message on the wind
To all the people that have sinned
For true love

Through the chimney pots there gleamed
A breaking dawn that seemed
Our own awakening
And as I kicked a can into the gutter
I heard you mutter
"That's broken the dream for me now!"
Hand in hand we walked alone
So both went off to our respective homes
How...our arms stretching wider wider wider
You to yours and me to mine
Separated now till another time

A white cloud billowed up above
Some stragglers fell out of a pub
Staggered off singing a song
While in that vapour
The idea formed aloud along
We'd have to meet now in a crowd
As to meet alone we would be prone
We couldn't face our own disgrace
Committing things
We both believed were wrong

Why cant we be bad
Its very very very sad
Its like there's us and
All the world's around us
Surrounds and hounds us

When we reached home
We stood over our beds alone
And said something inside our heads
Which I will never know you said
I keep to it but hope instead
When all is said and done
You make your bed and sleep in it
That legendary pun

ON A NEEDLE

The moon shook then shimmered in the brook
Injected on my page a look and grace beyond me
As I later tried to think about make sense of
And sketched nocturnal-ink visions into my musing book...

Out of the corner of my eye in water space
I saw a sizeable fish rise seemed to tease me to the chase
And the hunter in me was seized
Placing the book between my knees
I considered how to tackle and deliver fly and cast
Inadvertently gazed for a fast second at the moon
Don't know why

Where in its reflection shone out an old man's face
And bored through a surrounding silhouette
Of thorn like some border sewn in lace
The face looked deep into my soul

And in its expression held something of my late father's disdain
How could I cause such disturbance to a tranquil scene
His sardonic arched brow suggested and
Cause such an innocent creature pain

The earth I stood on also shook in this corner of Crookwood
Where water blasts a cut so deep beguiles the size of the river Wort
Where splashed my Wolfdane Crook
So I lay down on the dusty green sand squirmed a bed and sunk in
The soft leaf mould dirt and rotted oak leaves there and took stock
Up above me screamed an owl in the distance yelled a fox
And right beside me a badger growled as it fought long worms

And vibrations of love and awe throbbed through me
As I got up and strolled about in the moonlight
To clear my head under a dream of revolving milky frozen starlight
I took time to wander by my boiling stream as it too churned cream To wey and white

Out of the sky from behind a cloud bright Jupiter sprang
And Saturn Terracotta Mars following and ahead Venus all aligned
Created like a monotonic music bar up in the heaven

And so too a speck of Golden dust beyond
Sparked Mercury by a magic wand
I dizzily Craned behind me to see
Lighting up my path prelate to some damascene momentary sight

Then suddenly I tripped and fell backwards
And grasped at all the planets in my flight
But held only air and plunged helpless in the stream
All about me flashed bubbles in a frosty swirl
And silver bodies racing past fast gleamed

All at once one great fish blindly soared and smacked into my head
Forcing it and me to wake and I was pulled up through the surface From
Where I groped in slow motion in a reverie on the water bed onto Ground
If I'd floundered much longer surely I'd be dead and drowned
As I spluttered for my breath I regained my senses on the meadow Grassed shore
Your image lay there smiling maternal like some goddess arms Outstretched
As out the clutches you had pulled me from
Stuck to deaths beguiling molasses
And so I loved you even more

And as I choked yet caught some air flooding back to me
Not just this perilous chance I had diaried down but
Before one which recently I had encountered
Whence earlier on a needle
A magnificent trophied fish had fought

And I had bought the writhing muscle time
By heed debating on this its struggling life
And then deciding to inflict it would be indeed such a crime
And that I oughta with respect
Gently release it back in to the racing water

55

MY SWEET JASMINE

I close my eyes and strain to find
Something floating in my mind
In swirling bulbous clouds of grey
A slit like wound watches the day

I climb out of my rocking chair
I catch that scent pervades the air
Tingles rising neath my hair
Suddenly makes me aware
I look around and stare and stare and stare
She's not there the fragrance spent soon went
Appears a black speck miles away
Way high up in the sky
A hawk like shape a cover up
Becomes a pair of tiny lips
Tight unsmiling adamant

It has an air of seriousness

Below as in their separate squares
Dance a pair of ravelled hares
Display their bouting jousting wares
They spar the air and filibuster
Shadow boxing with their dusters
In the middle of my field
Sunken in this Wiltshire wealde
In and out new swallows swoop

In the backdrop roe deer stoop in

Cuckoo's pint while cuckoos piping
Drenched buttercups and nettles loop
Downstage newborn lambs a gambolling
Getting caught in briars a rambling briars
Rambling rambling in and out a barbed wire fence
What is the difference rambling briars
Where rabbits run and pheasants coop
Cunning tease a poachers pouch

Dewy lustre sprays about sleeping forms
Where leverets crouch
Lidless eyes stare hypnotised
Round and round and round they brink
Around a fire some mystics think
Until the bloody sunset sinks
And I sit back and sing my song
Where has my sweet pale yellow
Winter Jasmine gone

I tried to bring her back to life
Willing her return from death
And breathed my air into her mouth
But she faded nonetheless
In my arms my heart's caress
I am empty I am left
Like a mothering bereft.
'Cept this residue of song
Where has my sweet Jasmine gone

ORION'S SWORD

I had a vision I suppose
For a purpose to transpose
Some words into a song along
Where Angel's kiss conspires to miss
Where my bucolic youth has gone
A vision of a sword that
Hung down from Orion's belt
So young and strong shines
He his mettle never melts
He brandishes it reaps and cuts
At shadows of a love he's lost

Yet I too like him has sores
Which as I hurt ravish his heart
From a maiden now dissolved
Once in distress who bid me aid her
Now ignores the work
I've done she blessed
Who steps back in the darkness
So ego less

Whose fading image once
Furnaced like exploding coals
Which smote but now smoke out
As reticent fires about me die
He though still confounds
All odds as in some rage
Hurls great meteors at the Gods
Which sometimes fall down
Upon this little earthen sod

And below we opened mouthed gaze up as
Descending gold dust swirls
Reflects with awe what's going on light-years
From our world

He had a heart that wept not
But as the day approaches near
His chivalry accords that as the night recedes
The mighty hunter falls upon his fading sword

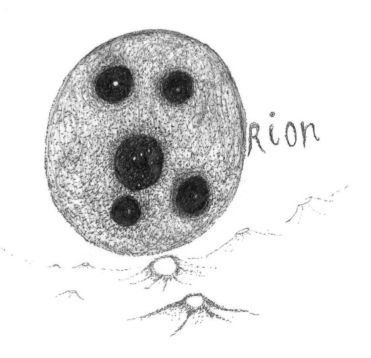

PAINTED LADY

Hi Ho Painted Lady
Silver maiden blonde an' lazy
Roll around in chromed gravey
Makes the sundial turn crazy
Stirs the dawns dust hazy mercury
Names sounds like electric cadence
Flying out of purgatory

She set light to in her stomach
Fireworks which made beacons flummoxed
Guided by a milky way
Staring up and miles away
She crept out searching
Stars to send to
Seeds of hers beyond her ken to
Fertilise in a cocoon

On past Mars and Pluto's moon
Through debris left in solitude
Charon steers her on the Styx
But lends his pole and bag of tricks
To knock her past the gravity felt
And on beyond passed Kuiper belt
No mingling with his mournful souls to
Circumnavigate black holes
When it lands her heart will flutter by
A gentle and ephemeral butterfly

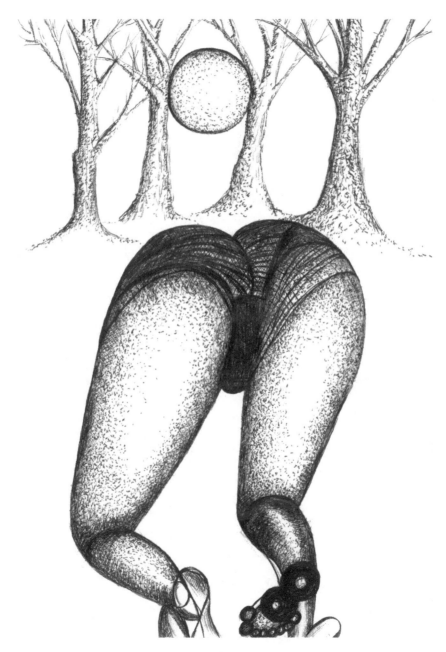

POOL OF LOVE

As your finger twists
Inside a golden ring
I dream of diamonds out
Of reach the stars recede
Beyond my touch which
I would like to place upon

But if I save up all my dreams
And sell them to the god who sees
Who writes down everyone of
Those people I have been with
And dispensed without a word
Maybe my hearts yearning
Can be served

I have fashioned from
Something written in my soul
Circles in a trembling pool of love
Eluding me creep back and forth
Across the surface
Then depart stretching to
True hearts but never
Melting into one

Catching the tail
Of a racing comet
As it disappears
Behind the setting sun
Hold those sparkles for my love
And cast them far
Exploding showers of meteorites
Little dusts descending from above

On everyone
But me

I wish that I could brush a stroke
To do justice to an ash and oak
Which lean as one so grown together
They are arm in arm
As I look to the dying sun
At two lovers' silhouette

Underneath their mighty boughs
Just before the bats awake
A flycatcher hovers now
Taking insects on the wing
And sipping Guinness from a tin
I look on laid on some hay
I've gathered in the gloaming

The cows and sheep
Sleep saying nothing
Fling myself spread
Out and splayed
As life's bothers subside
Their sting has gone
I've ceased to wade
Through memories
My mind resists
Its roaming
Until another day
My day is done
I am not half
Now I am one

PRAYER OF AN EARTHLING

Written in your eyes now
And again in your palm
A reading of alarm sounds in
The recital of some psalm

Though your silence is golden
Doesn't mean it cant do harm
See the mist across your fields
Hides broken promises to farm

An abduction of the truth
And all relating bacchanale
Spread declining acceptance
To a paucity of love

The destruction of your face
Spell concavances to charm
Merely famine true feeling
Making some sort of drama

Please don't believe me
When I say you are done
It is the doubt of lesser mortals
The misgivings of your son
My sun

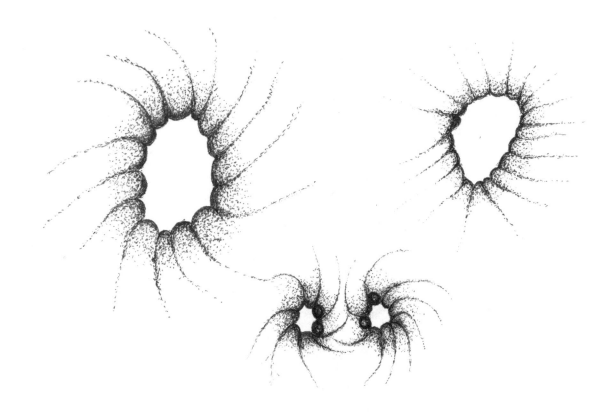

M W 2014

PLEASE KEEP SAFELY
IN YOUR HEART THIS LOVE OF MINE

In this life there is but little time
...And like some planets in a tryste align
A string of pearls disappear across
A solar system in relative space compared to time
As our souls do yours and mine
In spheres of ferocious light
Upon each planet its sun does shine
If I cannot have your love for mine
Then can I pray
Your love is divided equally to those who you confine
For in that equality I feel that I can find
Some solace in that your love for me
For no other does outshine

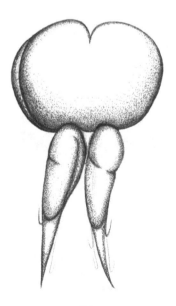

THE CORACLE

Sprinkling frankincense and myrrh
And sparkling like the stars out there

Everywhere the eye can see
Are smells that linger on the tongue
Gravitational waves from
Every single one of us
That venture near the sun are rent
And when the light has died and gone
The soul of it now carries on
Reflecting in those eyes which shone
Blinking every now and then where
Time and space are bent

The sunset's turning pink
The goodly shepherds turn to drink
To keep away the cold and think
That they are growing now too old
To keep an eye on our young fold
It's turning cold
There's red sky in the morning
Gives the shepherd's warning

A boat full of tears made of skin
That steered towards the chosen one
Careers and runs aground so thin
It leaks and sinks into the lake
So still the nuns have turned to stone
Yet droning on and on and on
They chant a sad relentless song

That sounds like wind rush in the grasses
Their time is almost done with sin
The sun and sex and turning pink

They twist their granite cowls which crease
Like brittle towelled cracking fleece
Their hair falls down as if released
As they turn they ask someone
Where have all the young men gone
But they appear a string of runes
Taller than a mans fortunes
Telling them to settle where
The soundscape turns and sinks

Organ fugues play on the breeze
For only kind words tease
Remind us what we want to think
Or was it all because of drink
Why all our thoughts were out of sync
The mindset's turning think

All in all its all the one
So one of us is all of them
And though there may be few survive
That's all there needs to be
The u and me
To keep us all alive
The seeds of you and I
You see the sunset's turning pink

THE FISHING

Even on a dull day
When trees so grey and threadbare
As dipped in molten lead
Bent inside out in an ill wind
Stalk like ghosts instead
Great heavy boulders
Of cloud in a bad mood
Bounce inside my brain
Knock my thoughts about
With no peace they shout insane things
Again and again and again
Ideas raining rhyme discords
In my head

Check the wind the mackerel cast
Like the buzzard in the sky thrown spirals down
Obscured by heavy blur
When odours of stale memories fill my mind
When ivy's hang obscure my view
Down a dark corridor I queue
And the knife cuts crudely through
Stale crusts of bread my thoughts dispersed
Crumbs spread cascade get everywhere instead
And unread newspapers
And all that's left on an unmade
Lonely dank bed-only an old empty marmalade jar
My star the sun moves in the dusty silenced room imitates
A womb where grows
The tortoiseshell moments of a winter sunset
Twinkles as it rolls it tinkles as it spins sped- kicked irritably
Across
A cold floor stops abruptly and lies stone-dead

You stir my mental eye
Though I maybe gagged dumb and speechless
Really I am singing under this canopy of wintertime
I am guided by the things you've said
Later I will form the words thumping in my head
Sculpted in dispatches to someone else who heard
Related to the world and all there are to hear
I see a shadow stir inside a willow's roots
Snatches on its flank of glimpses of the blinking sun
Dark shape come to where I angle
Under translucent hazy moonlights
Where salix and bulrush ravel arms a tangle
On these cloudy days and opaque crystal nights
Radiating rain splashing weakly washes
My recoiling face
Like a Bacon paint to paste
Your emblazoned scales a myriad flashing
Of bubbles suddenly festooned
Down my impotent naked barren fields and trees I stride
You are the only fertile thing

Aching in the wet breeze the stream arches up to meet
Which sharpens my mind your constant waters
Bending falling fish
My hands bloodless fingertips
Grip white and red the springed stringed rod
I search for pike on the brown leaf coloured murky Wylie
Over hangs the stream bed sodden bank slips
Where they like to lurk and slyly loiter where coots lisp

By the spraints of otter trotting rotting moister
Freshening my hands and lapping nibbling at my feet
Minnows scarper like sprinkled gold dust
Where the water boils across this leat

That sudden draw on line-life jerked
Paroxysm of the chase the sudden sweat
And hair rise on my neck ricochets down my spine
So instantaneous no time to double check
The tug of a hooked thing so responsive complete
Conducts a tameless puppet on a whining string wild random flings
Throwing all these thoughts around an empty dish
Cavorting in a swirl tossing all your weedy curls about
Transported on a cold sour wind all my hidden sins
Pulls away from me desperate on my screaming reel
My taught and snapping tendon cord stretches even more
Then as suddenly flaxes relaxes slack
The heavy burden now like dead weight
Spent after fighting rolls like a whale ashore

All the things I've ever done
Suddenly explode and shine
Suspended in this time I've won
From you my lord

THE FROZEN WALK

As I leapt across the stile the sun broke through awhile
Across these fields so crisp and shone with frost my boots slipped
On the frozen icy step I had climbed upon
I gazed into that fierce ball all blurred white
And gold exploded spun
I lost my footing at a cost collapsing wood and wire and the sheep Rushed up to see
The puddles translucent like porcelain plates smashed to break my fall
Dusted down the frosted spray caught the wind like diamonds and Blew away
And in the vacuum left inside my mind my perception blinded
The memories rushed back in as the sharp cold pinched the skin

A red fox clean rangey rare and lean with gorgeous sheen
Stared in shock at me and held one paw
Dithered as it sniffed the air
A pheasant in its mouth still moving as it struggled helplessly
Those colours on a palette all blended into one
And I marvelled at this pastiche in the dying sun

I glanced up as the clouds grew like a darkened brow
And in a second knew the snow was coming
How thick and fast so suddenly so silently
And on this frozen scape would come to last
Much longer than the revelry that held me in its grasp

I realised my wrist was snapped my heart leapt
The fox sprang back down into the winterbourne off at a lick
Its thick brush flicked a trail in the white coating
The sheep in danger threat smote the ground with their tiny hooves...
Then ambled away in the snow now laying on a meandering path

72

Pain was creeping like a fire up my shattered arm fast
So bound it with some string and elastoplast I kept for just in case
And all the while I couldn't shake that image of your face that followed me
Always admonished me so coquettish and cajoling made me
Warm in this arctic place.

A buzzard slid from a tall oak where it'd hid and let out a mew... glid
Which echoed in the vale and bid farewell like a tolling bell
As the bough its perch snapped and fell

Right into my eyes the fox's stare had transfixed me
And I let out a gulp of air I had held in for some time
The vapour rolled like smoke
And deep within a voice spoke

Remember these days when country folk and wild creatures still
Hunter gathering exist subsist alongside fill larders with
Firewood apples cherries walnuts hazel sweet berries and their crops
They keep their counsel and their stock
Live off the land with game and grains in summer and in wintertide

Abide with me fast falls the eventide...soft hymn sung in my head
I looked over at my cabin sat fat in this scene with its snowy thatch
Like a chocolate cake
The walking wounded ...I held on to an oaken shaft
Sloped off to my bed

THE MAIN SONG

I can hear a thousand voices talking fast
They fall softly at first upon my roof
Tinkling as they race down the gutter in the rain
I can hear the raindrops like tiny bells

Tintinnabulation falling whispers
Tickling trickling laughing
Creating music as they ring
Sing out swirling down the drain

Then they have done
Silence... rain is gone
I imagine the sky has broken wide
The morning's come

Criss cross the broken pencil scratches
Rakes a mark upon the page
There I sit beside the crow
Like my old school teacher
Looking down its nose at me
Below

Criss cross your twisted buttocks
Cross the floor off for a pee
Like a pair of walking scissors
Back again to me
The day goes bang and across the crack
Red as far as the eye can see

Where the eye bleeds sunset spreads
But the blood dries black
From the east a silhouette

A 'v' of geese
Shoots like an arrow head toward
The bulbous perigree orb
Punctures the moon of moons
Fireworks explode and shower down
A salvo of silver spoons

Grabbed at one
Had a bowl of flakes
As the night world wakes

I left my bed under the howling sky
A rapprochement between you and I
Went walkabout...
Not sure if it was me or the sky
Howling like a lonesome wolf
Too old for all this
You're too young for I

I wondered why
The bed was bare
Save a hair dark lying there on the pillow
Walked out to the fields - chased the dawn
Lay down -the only dark form
Lying on the yellow

Too cold on the cut field
And I had a drink
From the Crookwood stream
Yeah? Nice thought but
More likely the Butler/Belfast sink- I think
Cooler inside the shed - than out

Couldn't sleep for images causing turmoil down
The drain I call my mind
Filtered through my mental marl
My limbs creaking in the frosty atmosphere
And in my head wanted time to rationale

Settled there felt the rush of hair brush my
Thinning a while a rhythm patina
My ageing stasis at
In a crisis
My life acquiescence
I have a dream I jump a stile
My feet paddling with you in that
Smiling sun-splashed stream

A view from space
The creased frozen face of a Don Cossack
Lost on a Siberian arctic landscape
It looked like the underneath
Of a fallen leaf

And made me wonder why the pigeons flew away
A stray cat or hungry fox
Or merely a tiny dormouse rustling as it
Revolves
As it sleeps in a frosty box
Something
Triggered their clocks

Larger beings float in space
View our place where we sit knitting
Patterns of our short lives
If they visited from outer there
What of their beliefs - a vox populi?
Seeing low grasses where we see trees
I got down on my knees like a lion would
Testing the air

Would they be able to hear and see...
See us simply as we see ants
And bees and wasps and fleas
Like this lady bird lost
Crawling up the frost encrusted stalk
In front of me
And treat us just the same
Like we that cannot see...

A mismatch suggesting
Whales and plankton in the sea

A million strings sprang up like thunder
You strode into the moonlight pool
That evaporated as the clouds came in
In prelude to the lost song

Rains were coming
And as you sang and danced
Across the Kalahari tundra terrain
Horns from migrating bovine beasts
And pachyderms chasing the rain
Joined the strings in a lightening clap of thunder

Out to the ruined fields again
We tread
Where once elephants had crops stampeded
And poachers lay in wait with ivory toffs
Clutching their Kalashnikovs
Our forms lay in narrow beds surrounded by buttercups
In the long meadows by a sleepy church
And a floating winding stream

But always I escape and dream
I search you to come to join me
Mabon maiden and as you wane
With ivory breast and strawberry mane
You metamorphose into the dark haired Samhain

And how can all that be wrong
Another muse for me again
No pity for no sin

Humming a tune now
Softly crept softly past the empty pews
The holy smell of candles burnt
In the cool transept
I ask again- I'll ask forever in that song
I peruse
As I turn the frozen leaves of a hymn book
In Urchfont church
Reading words I do not use
Near where my fallen Angel
Belongs

Once more out in the day
The cattle chomp and the scent of hay
The mists swirl the late lark rises up
As a plane would lost in fog droning
Wings like props
Purring whirring
Till just a speck
And though her voice lingers on
She has gone
On her last song

I think of my lover philandering
Controlled by her phone
Just like a drone flitting from one to the other
Texting thinking laughing but...

Nothing is up there with the Angels
One messenger appears through
The weak sun's haze
Knocks on my door without fail
Like the postman with today's mail
Blowin' on his pink hands
As houses appear to him out the fog
You're next door
Your the next one

And so it goes on till all us are done
That's the main thing
In the last song...

And one day as autumn fell back in shed leaves to be a fall
Across those emerging swirling fields I heard the call
Time crying to be installed
But its so fleeting it was blown out in a misty squall
And in the end eternity beat it up an' all

As a shrouded sheep coughed on a fallen apple core
In the orchard where I sit
And contemplate it
My small flock lie steaming in the sun stewing
Time time time it ticks away
Ears flicking
Tags clicking
Now more than ever as nothing's doing
It called me out
Drew a line through the woods
Along which I crawl

An ancient crack twixt two limestone cliffs
A cathedral space caused by iceflow then drovers
Sheep and cattle drives consumed by many feet
Fluted ivy columns and interlacing boughs meet
Fan vaulted

Great beech rooted bare trunks
Where woodpeckers drill in still hours drunk
Their echo plays like hollow organ pipes
Reaching to a canopy above swirl ecclesiastical airs
Where fly angels bill 'n cooing like wild doves

The circle at the bottom of this chamber
Caused by the sunken lane below and arboreal surround
Frames as I look back and down the hilled track a picture
Hitched to an old fence stick with a rusty nail
Of that distant vale of Potternewick

Creates a stained glass window some what cracked
By withered branches across a pane
Of time suspended like in aspic as it's blurred
The many souls who've laboured up through these Folly woods

Voices heard I stop
And whispers live- hear now
Dialects of earlier times
When the fallen from the plague
Were carried buried on the field above
In three mass graves
Their faces never show but etched
In gnarled trunks and twisted roots
They last

Not many leaves cling on now anyhow but enough to cause a stir
Murmured in the air which whistles as it descends a wretched oboe
Down from the brow the far off sound of roosting crows
Shadow figures tread softly bent in patched robes and
Fraying cowls praying
Mingle forever with the eerie screech
Of hunting owls

'STICKY WICKET' M.W. 2019

Breaking outside this air is fresh and sounds much wider
An idling tractor growls low
A hare breaks cover and scuds across the cut corn
That loose panther ready to strike
Up shoots the moon like a prowling eye
And again the owls hoot

Stubble turns red and blue in the sunset
The crows sleep mist creeps
Kaleidoscopic colours sweep then seep
Weep
Drip drop drip fill the sense
The terrible beauty
A pheasant shot and forgot
Hangs on a barbed wire fence

And one day
Along the way
Back in summer
Long gone
Where we lay in the tossed hay
Or sheltering from the rain
My head on your lap lost in love
You stroking my thinning hair
Without a pain without a care
In the main
I write this song

THE MAN IN THE MOON

As fast as the eye can see
I chase his reflection following me
I swim in circles I'm all at sea
While the man in the Moon
Watches over me

Treading water trying to breathe
While the Man in the Moon
Goes behind a cloud
Shouting shouting shouting loud
In the muted ear of a silent crowd

Motionless I'm stranded
Under the night sky
Yet the Man in the Moon
Just sails on by

I stroked the blackbird on her nest
The Man in the Moon is growing less
Before he fades behind the Sun
He blesses me for what I've done

She lightly pecks my finger tips
What wondrous thing such friendliness
Such fidelity when petrified
I'd chased away the magpie pest
And stare into those moistened eyes
Darker than the starry sky

I wanted you so badly
What if you flew away
While there at home you rest
Oblivious I expect

Getting some hard earned sleep lest
An uphill struggle through the day
You have to cast idle thoughts
Of me away

As the morning intensifies black to blue
Only streets away from me you
See the same sky which I see
Drawn by lunar passions too

May the Man in the Moon smile down on you

THE MOUNTAIN TOP

I've always thought about the hills
And mountain tops when mental ills
Befall
A mountain climb's a bitter crawl
But seemingly a better pill
And later physic to my will
To be
So often climbed up to a crest
Which seems to alleviate
The best of hurts that beset me

Turn my face into the sun
Or rain if that is the terrain
Blindly trundle on
As fog descends and all grows silent
Save the mournful bleat
The echoing thud of my close feet
The feather soft footfall of the sea mists'
calm

The solstice sun
Burns through and suddenly I meet you
And look about north west east and south
Where have you come from spectred sight
You're form exploding through the light
I take breath out from your moist mouth
Your softly spoken words anointing growth
Sit on a cairn and yearn for your return
Realising that after running repairs
Still I'm blessed able
To reach such lofty heights

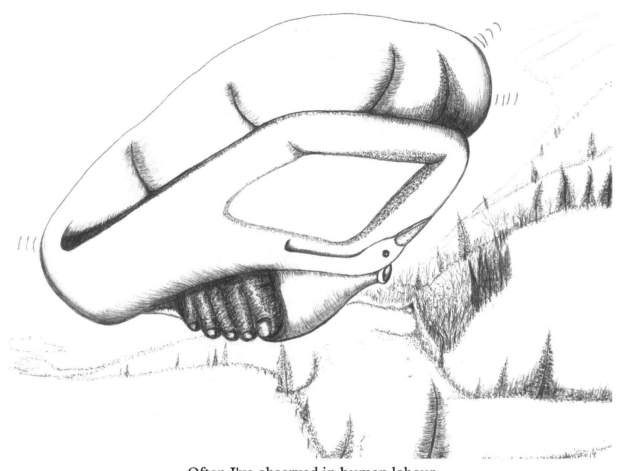

Often I've observed in human labour
Through your clinging vapour
Though obscuring views
Faces filled with glee of some family
Who've persevered to reach the top...
Their happiness affecting me
I hope it never stops how nature brings together
All us birds of a feather

Now disappear all mens' slights and niggling
Belittling fears no forms need fittling
As over there in sheer mid-air
The raven and the buzzard seer
Tumbling in a fight to see
Whose is this majesty

Metaphorically and physically
I'm stood above the crowd of tittle tattle
Human battles rage below
No sound of traffic or cries or barks
Just the ever-present effervescent lark
Reaching its zenith

And as the sun goes down
It kisses ranges peaks and crowns
Distant cattle and sheep shun sleep
Graze on, drowned in the silver light
The ancient Strawberry moon stretches up
Gazing upon and revelling in the sight

Glazing dew tinkling kinetically in late breezes
Casting a million strawberry droplets
As far as the eye can see
Igniting the far off church clock pauses
Then solemnly strikes one
Enough to cause bats dispersal
Its golden weather vane cock silently crowing

In the corner of the eye like
Some omen from the sky
Showers of meteors fly
Then abruptly die pink
Rose petals floating down to earth
Caught in flight and in sync
Pathways illuminate and awakened
Ghosts of walkers emblazoned
Chance the ephemeracy of night

Flanks of fells and screes
Tease the eye to please
Where uproarious clouds
Billow the size of mountain sides
And rains fall fountains
Of becks furiously milky-white
Ghylls foam and rumble
Down to quiet tarns humbled
And if you listen closely
The babbling water
Tumbling disturbing pebbles
Spins a diatribe
Of human yarns

THE NIGHTMARE

I crept into the wood one night
So quietly to hide because
Life had become a bad dream
A nightmare
My thoughts inflamed so ravelled
And intangible too loud to say
I had decided where wary of the day
My opened mind might fall prey

I walked past giant roots that grew from stricken
Oaks which once threw great shadows
Now woodpeckers patterns had pointilised with holes
And deep into their moss laden
Orifice my mental juices flowed
My mind grew images of huge hairy elephants at play
That wrestled in that secret pond in days of yore
At night together over there
And tore and did sink with their massive
Tusks into this very clay I think
Woolly rhinoceros and shaggy bison rutted here
And came to drink

The land had glutted with such wild preposterous things
And burrowed souls of ancient badger lives
Passed on down centuries where they stayed
When sable wolves and silver foxes came
And went and in the air near
I caught the sense that some still wandered here
Left alone and free where dwelt the spirits of old woods

And as I trod a branch gave way below my feet
Snapped I tripped and fell hard
When I woke I shook myself and shocked a voice said
"You are not forbidden you're very welcome here!"
Then from a shadow formed from I felt a spalpeen or a sprite
Appeared a figure slight of someone I once knew
Lit only by a glow worms light came through anon
From years ago they had returned
As I wrestled with memory burned
A stretched out comely hand
Beside me stayed me walking on

The moon broke through a cloud
Like some damascene moment all came clear
Revealed her face so lovely and
Like the planet Jupiter shone beside so near
She touched my cheek then gently kissed my lips
To test if I was real

My heart increased its pace then raced
Until whole seasons passed a year at least
And in that space leaves burst out of buds
Then shrivelled in cruel frosts
In between the sky fell in then rose and flew
On winds ill which rocked this ill fated place
That lifted leaves suns and moons
Rains drummed down relentlessly and swamped
Like a hurricane the whole ground monsooned was pulled up
Then dropped like a helpless ship on violent waves

As I ran about I fell and grasped at snake-like briars
In my striving to escape I thought my wired brain would burst
Before I got out this angry malevolence
Trains blew and whistled down the wind like sirens carrying sins
Trees creaking cracked leapt up and smote the ground rended
Thunder grew abounded sounded lightening ripped and bright as a day
I shouted in my pain as thorns plucked and scratched my face
The wind tore the roof off my mouth as I fought to flee this place
And bent the trees forever in that wood till at last in a great gasp
Blew out raging all went still

The vision re-emerged and once again
My heart surged but this time
She snatched me by my hand
As in a vice then oh so soft
I felt all time was lost
She smelled of earthy things
A dearth of scent and spice
Just simple blossoms
She was sweet...she was nice
She shook her hair and stars came out
And night things flew about

We slipped down to a stream
And as in a dream we tossed and bathed
My heated brow that sweated so
"Now now now" she whispered
She calmed somehow I let her know
We clung together so long we melted into one form
And slipped below the surface where
The splendid pulsating stars reflected now
We rose and caught our breath
I promised her I would come back again

Then let her hand go

I heard her cry then my echo
"Come back come back come back!"
The golden pool in lunar rays began to turn then spin
Turned silver as it spun till at length I landed with a thud
Alone upon the leaf-mould ground I looked around
As one would alone once more except
I heard her sing a song and laugh which faded
Like the nighttime in that early morning air
What had just passed was dawning on me
But no one there save a punctured shadow
The outline of her figure over there
Now only an evaporating aura
A fox barked and an owl's muted hoot
She was fading in a smoking morn
Then gone

An equilibrium befell as I leapt up
A meteorite shooting star like a firework broke
Burst silently above I felt her face
Soft as a dove bore a smile like
An angel looking down on me
Familiar became this midnight glade of omens
My thoughts raced round love
As it does when one dreams of someone
It changes them somehow
My feet in tandem quickened too
I looked about and realised
For years I'd dreamt of this place
And now it had come true

I gazed at all that nature held as I briskly walked away
And wondered at those things that pass
Across these fields and woods that cast impressions
Of this night and day
In peoples minds there must be others blessed
Of a greater lucid sagacious erudite kind than I
For what must have trespassed and
Transpired in nights of theirs
For I am just an ordinary guy

But suddenly I was running and dawn
Broke fast chasing at my heels
I had become clear minded
My heavy thoughts had fled
All about me felt really real
And indeed I had no longer
Doubt or needed more to feel

THE ROE DEER DOE

As I turned a corner in Potterne wood
Just by a tumbled down ruin where once a gamekeeper's cottage stood
The sun burst through and burned and branded
The patterned shadow of the web-like trees above
Where years they'd anciently rocked groaning
And tossed their tousled locks in winds yet
Had stood their ground now full grown and caused this glade
Suddenly before me laid out as on a distinct cold humus plate
Bright green shoots of grass and bluebells would in April May prelate
That weaved a bright carpet of emerald food where nimbly grazed a doe

I heard the familiar sounds of the vale below of my mate Stuart Brown down
Where his digger piping reversed in distant fields
The fitful haunting whine of a chainsaw wielded by gamekeeper Barry Hunter
Filtered across where Gordon Straker's farm lay in poplars shielded
Then some dogs barked in play as Nicky walked them out but in an opposite way
Fading on the wind

She the doe half stirred and tested with her senses but digested knew it meant
No harm today so far off were they
Me behind her stock still would be her only foe here in this wood
And in me like a hunter in the past rose primeval instincts
For we forget we are descendant animals and still retain in our blood
Those strains we now reign in

A rogue mustard cloud crept overhead and burst in huge drops
The splatter of an April shower
Procured a strong breeze that across me sped up wind of this graceful deer
That bowed her head and raised it chewing and treading daintily
Who just as suddenly caught my scent and turned around and as if I'd meant to Sin
Her wide shocked innocent eyes held me in its amazed gaze awhile

In that second I recalled the look upon a girl far away in Africa one day who I had
Come upon in the bush while hunting with my camera for a decent shot
Picking berries in a rush who trespassed on some game lodge plot
Who turned and panicked to run off but I pushed my finger to my lips and smiled
She impishly laughed high like some tropical bird and hovered for a second beguiled
Before she disappeared looked round with that look of recognition and blew me
A kiss which melted my heart

Some lifted raucous rooks broke crying sharp and departed alarmingly
When like a rifles crack from that old rocking canopy upstairs flew a mighty bough
A branch which dropped so fast and in a dusty blur how
It gave the cowering creature such a whack it felled her stunned
I rushed to the spot and in a frenzy not knowing my own strength lifted the bough
And wrestled to free the forlorn wretch on which rotten wood
And all amount of debris settled bedded so still I thought her dead and shouted
But with great relief at length she upped stumbled like a new born shook and
Scampered a few paces then turned about to me
And I'm sure in those doe-like eyes she smiled blew me a kiss
So sweetly beguiled and bounded off

THE WOODS

I don't know if I ever should
Go back again to Potterne woods
Great breathing mass of crinkled trunks
Where cow's breath lisps
Goldfinch kiss in wild plum blossom

And in natures fecund bosom
The bullfinch eye revolves to see
Elderberry laced berries squeezed
In the boundary hedgerows thorned
Where blasts the long gone
Echo of a hunting horn
Its mate hypnotised
Its red breast teased
Accompanied by that solitary wheeze
Dugs and udders full of honey
Milked by droning hairy bees
Their bellowed legs and poking noses
Violating foxgloves sleeves

Sunny shafts which cast
Long shadows dying ease
Birdsong sunk in crisp crenulated
Rusted human junk
Lowering voices crept and slunk
Where many ghosts stalked where I stood
Then, and more of mine now creep
Steeped in evocation lay the souls
Of rendezvous where couples stole
Ideas rarely realized

Cast in bronzed steel
Melted only real in dreams
Lotions spread as many as the
Bluebells carpet patina patterned glades
Notions never finished
Under that canopy so cool
And lurking shadows spring and fade
The arsonists and vandals wade
And dance orgiastically in shade

I promise you I made and broke alas
Love I spoke of some invoked
But more just thoughts which perished
By that wayside path

The characters in those limestone cliffs
The train rattling, shunting
Dredging sleepers from their beds
Where the vale falls away
Down westward strays

Then at midnight when the nestled
Wombs of badgers bunkers
Call out to the flowery dells with unguent
Pungent acrid smells
Of tissue blood and bone
And scare the nodding azure heads
In misted nickel wakening threads
Twine regal glory round your throne
Wild woodbine lingers then is gone

Tread softly in this holy sanctum
Cathedral like its plangent silence
Reverberates down its cloistered violence
Hallways rising to the dome
By fluted columns ash and oak
Dawn awakes its home and broke
Omnipotent there you stand alone

Yet pigeons mournful
Blow muted clarinets
And pheasants bluster splutter
As they escape their penning nets

While their keeper's flashing sapphire eyes
Search signs of fox where vermin lies
Raises his amulet

Straying there a while
I sometimes stop upon the stile
A smile comes but then it goes
And memories grow fly on the wind
And die as on it blows
Show to me life's necromances
Ephemeral highs and
Those long lost chances
No body really knows.

THERE WAS A DAY

There is a day that roasts in spray and early mist - where forced
A waters trace is caught and boils in sunlight - on a frosty morning
Where a wagtail darts up to catch 'fore I can think-a single ink
Blue bottled fly - even in wintertime
Built there with sore hands and knees and back and hips I bore
Underneath the waters slips a bridge of wood-discarded lengths
Stands spans the banks totalling more than the sum of their strength
To ferry across sheep and me and hound

I clutch at grasses on my way down
To sit and dangle as a kid - my legs
Just to prove I still can at my age -and recall the pure simple pleasure to relate
To see what it once was like to be again - so small
I gaze as if for the first time at all the sloe - or blackthorn - fast to the mast
Which later blossoms with no equal from the tight spiky thicket-cast
And watch the steaming breath of my sheep as they lick-it
To get an icy drink upon and sate their flicking demonic tongues between

And further up downstream from the spate too long ago I sat-late
Waiting with patience as a virtue for familiar blond hair to appear
Like bounced back shards of splintered sun
As in a virtual perfect honeyed moon looked down and smile-undone
From silver turned and wrought by our own soft love our teeth
Shone so wide we nervously sought out each other's souls inside

That holding hands we dropped so gently bent and retrieved some glass
We found it half-buried in the worn pebbles on that stream bed
Undid the top and poured as if all over our new world a balm
Like the sun gleams on a melted droplet in this melting
Frost from a tiny empty jar

YOU WISH

...I wish I could knock lightly
on your half opened door
step softly to your warm bed
kiss you gently on your silent lips
and quietly leave for ever

...Your hand barely holding
a crumpled tissue
your saintly brow relaxed
from issue
just sleep suspended
you in form
before the days idea
dawns

...But I have hundreds
miles to ponder
the ever stretching road
out yonder and grinding
mindless thoughts
to keep me
from falling at
this wheel asleep

A WINTER MAGIC

Two streams of late...
A winterbourne once just a trickle
Along a ditch gains pace
Beside a winding track pours into
Joins forces with a rush
Deep swirls
Preprandial drink before it sinks
Over silver ice terrace slides
Eddies spiralling labyrinth

Thoughts gargle thawed from
Under frozen plates tinkle giggle chuckle
From out the back of Urchfont
Church lurch the Christmas singers
Unseen springs lingers
Races over rills and leats

Passed Stert and Sleight a spate
And through Ham Orchard
Shake the late
Fruit frozen hard buckled
Clinging to the trees
Like sugared sweets

Meet in a confluence of minds cast
And in the snow between they
Cut a stronger darker flow
Run mingled now a life blood pulse

Arteries blush with leaves and stains
Dark between black rocks
And under fallen oak
We stood white cloaked

Echoed once singing yarns
Now mummified wrapped up
Is just a croak
Muted ideas flake

Tumble from the leaden sky
Kiss the surface melt disappearing
As our memories do too
Under Crookwood

Past dormant mill slow and still
Round farm leaning
'Neath leaking thatch
Tilting growing more than built
Beards of wilting fronds slow the flow
Enticing waddling ducks
From their impenetrable pond

The brook
Courses on
Ricocheting
From banks off turns
Under low arches
Cracked edifice forgotten
Yawn steaming swim cattle sterns
Moored to rotten posts
And on across the fields
White pillowed
Punctured eiderdowns
Snow flurries spill
Pastures piqued out
A polar glow

Wobbles on to
Potternewick lit
Sunk in a wood smoke dusk
Meanders a while
Past fallen fence
Frozen heron
Stilted now
Stuck motionless
A husk abides
By watering hole clings
A static hunched up water vole
Eyes tight in blizzard stings
O'er stile
To Worton
Creeps
Where the
Weak sun
Succumbs

Sleeps
Streams
Of conscious
Falls into
Night
Dreams

SHE IS A WOMAN OF HER WORD...

Rolled up in this canvass
Absurd when it unfurled
Falling out I sang a song

Unwinding all my memories
Held in for so long
Across so many seas and lands

My face though weathered
Still... belonged
My hammock now slung
In the hollow of her hands

And there my trouble lies in
The thoughts behind my eyes

If you knew everything I did
You'd never do anything
You would never've come along

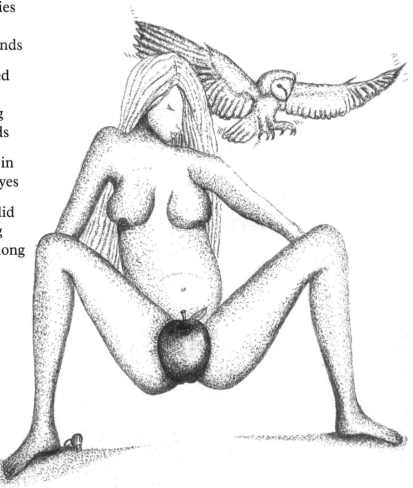

A Dream and No One Knew

I dreamt about you the other night
And I can feel you now
Everyone was there talking loud
But it seemed there was no one else about
And no one knew
I kissed your neck and you pulled me to you
It was like a dream come true
And I woke up just before it dawned on me
That none of this was true

So I thought I'd tell you
And ask if this
Had ever happened to you
And you'd dreamt about me too
And woke woken up confused
And how it wasn't true
If you can feel me now
And if it was a dream come true
And no one knew

AM ME

The sun wrestled the moon to the floor climbing
Like a light balloon...
I was watching a tiny orange spider
Tie a tight rope from a rose across the old stone paved path
To another bush...to where did it rush?
I could have brushed through it unawares
And snapped its micro gossamer twine
As it swung it crawled across the great divide
Determined on its line
I had driven earlier up over where the road
Crosses the Ridgeway track back near the ancient
Sanctuary where our ancestors passed along
...We are all going somewhere
Like a travelling song

Now if I glanced down along my
Numb tired arms resting
Away and up and above me
To the church tower burnt grey
And mottled lichen-yellow over many years
I lay like a cold tomb stained with years' toll
Swifts like black darts skimmed up high diving
Off the golden shoulders of slate-bellied nimbus
Penetrating my soul

Crumbling like a pitted cake sat St Johns
Where penicillin grows-spreads in moulding spots
How many candle's melted shine
On tongues held out to receive
Communion hosts and bread and wine
Louder even louder noise increasing all the time

An aeroplane in the distance getting closer all the while
And a drumming of propellers whipping round shook the ground
And I looked up at the spaces of the sun between the clouds
Of the azure all exploding and propellers going round
And I hovered in a revelry
My feet up off the ground

I allowed the sun to blaze down on me dozing
Thinking -my eyes tight closed
Like a tide a green light rose behind my eyes
Drowned and held my whole mind inside
The sunlight blurring my retina
Beneath my lids I slide

I left her bent over pruning
Clearing her nasturtiums of black fly
In amongst her painted tyres trailing
I could smell them on her
Peppery breath panting
As she wiped her brow and face
And set her hair by with grace
She had nibbled some while working there
And looking back seeing her
My heart leapt
My mind crept cautiously

Don't say anything wrong
Don't play to chance
Don't let her see you snatch a glance
Of her perfect form beneath the frock
Her slender flank of a supple kind
Bending now like she could perform
As if to take her from behind

107

Do not release your furtive thoughts to go there...
But they did
Don't incur that feisty wrath when mocked
To take off like a hell-bent whirring moth
Strip off that diaphanous floral frock
Film pulled off the spool within
Slim as a firework she personified vim
Her short fuse struck like petrolled cloth
That broke many of our rendezvous
Usually triggered by some booze
It doesn't have to happen
If I keep my cool

I raised my arm and cried goodbye
I saw her dart a glance my way
Over her shoulder
Just to check if I'd been bolder
But I didn't stay and looked away
No gaze no harm
And left her working all alone
At one within her pretty home

108

AND AS I LEFT

...and as I left the sunken lane went down
Down below the fields where cold sun white washed and slow ...
Multi pebbled strata stripe-chevron walled my cell
Like roots only my hair still grows
Quiet as a frozen orange thumb
Pondered on any hope
Rose again upon an organ note to the zenith of my fun
Streaks of melancholy won
Pushed up out the ground beech stallions with sparse matt copper leaves
Remaining stalked the all around
Bald grey brown black and pale the fields lay naked and undone
The winds swirled far up in a whirl wind
Lifting rooks dancing as demi semi quavers on paper music hangs...
On top a curling wave overpowered of laughter dive free
Willed into a swell
Then quiet as the evening creeps
As a stealth frost falls over everywhen

Then without occasion an invasion
As the ashen greyness splits like a blown on dead ember rips open into Vulcan smiles
The sky awakens its lids part

And the apposite in purple streaks and blushes
Run the beds of sunset berries nestled in the bushes
Ink indigo scrawled as written from a pen
Round the edges hedges lurk dark margins bordered crammed
With shadows dance excited finches through unupholstered twigs and thorn
Bare brazen pulchritude like the time to plant strawberries
Taken rubies from the charms which circumnavigate your slender wrist
The sun has become a burnished golden coin twisting out its snake skin
Of winters raw swollen ciste

Away from the Solstice

Walk off a well trodden
Dusty path tangentially to burnt grass
Off piste the goings tough the stuff is rough
Like a safari walk in Africa the dust kicks up
At every scuff
From Avebury to where Stonehenge lies
The sun is burning like a ciste

Land so dry its turned to crisp no sound
Save grasshopper's lisp
Always my eyes train the bushes and the bluffs expect to see
A mane arise and shake and yawn those massive teeth
Hypnotic eyes underneath sunk in my insides
Devour me while I'm still alive

You showed now - the pigeons rise
I know where you approach me from
Though I cannot hear them clap
Their wing beats in this heat the echo sapped
On your belly you surprise a myriad of butterflies
One flutters down a tiger moth
It lands upon your ferile nose
Its feathered wings blown inside out
In a dog fight
See it scream and writhe and shout
But no sound does come out
Hangs in its
Deaths pose
No help in sight

Soft underbelly of this valve
Across big billowing white ship cloud sail
I lay back in a dream upon a tartan rug
Quilted fields where in crop circles
Embroidered rotate and roll
The goodly people hug trees an' stroll

Stalked from up above a buzzard falls
And fells a collared dove scrolled
The blessing hand of god it seems absolving
A confetti battle of feathers spiral down
And as it rips out heart and soul
It leaves me empty I stare right into
The hunters eye a fathomless black hole
As near to nature as I feel
I am not of these harsh realities.

A childhood nightmare reoccurs
Freefalling down and with a jolt
Jettisoned from the throat of an evil she-wolf
In Afghan coat
Upon your back
Insects play hop scotch
Crack! a gunshot breaks the air
Sheep bolt and in that picnic site just there
Agoraphobic faces stare
That's where I go to stroke your hair
Somewhere where I feel more there

Beyond the fringe of avenues
Traffic queues honks and bleats
In cars on melted tar
Their backsides stuck to welded seats
Parents lance their chronic boils
The same as children eating sweets

And in the greater scheme of things
We're comforted by all our blings
The ring of stones we all go round
For centuries have made no sound
Round your wrist a bracelet hangs
Of moonstone imitation fangs
They stand together none the less
Monoliths adorned caressed

As a strawberry sun sets on our day
Bleeding now into the west
Into our nest we retreat
Your blood red lips my eventual treat
I see some guy wielding a pick
I smell a throng pull heavy stones
I hear the cries I feel the sighs
Lick my lolly on a stick
My head buried in your wide
Making love so hard somehow
We may come out the other side

BARNARD'S LOOP

In Orion
A melting quoit ionized loiters
Red mist hung like a noose

But Orion fights out of this strangle hold
The hunter breaking loose

Away from the cosmos and staring up
Under oak trestles proud
With green huile mouths
Tossed in northern winds
That wield to the south
Crows a mute girl with a silver smile
She craics
She leaps and sings as she eats some bread
But cannot find her voice
Instead
It turns to gold as she makes her bed
Andover head it is raining

But there- nothing in the breezes
Skirting the Vizes
To tell how my own hearts bleedin'
Chevrons chevrill as swallows dive
Over Imber's still glowing as crop fires die
And all of this caught in your eye
As a film preserved for étrangers

She grasps tiny cymbals between her fingers
She magics all of the wild flowers to tinkle
But they are only able to winkle
Tils head over heels in impish peals

A deaf Shrew tons at her noiseless squeals
Scurries away on speed
She sprinkles and sprinkles and sprinkles
Some fairy dust as it mingles
And in the air it catches the hair of a lunatic
Paddling in shingles

To his left he witnesses theft
By Bishops canning fruit
But the villagers learn
Are a thieving lot
And All cannings turn to loot

At Alton barns are burning
The locals they are yearning
Look up at the stars from
Their Bottlesford bars
Yet no sound's discerning

The madman with two roving eyes
And a Worton his nose
Which circulates round and round
Opens his mout' to mouth some words
But his tongue cant catch a sound

Over the ground by the Wotterne Pick
Near a Crooked wood called The Rook
Where eerie noises should emanate
Silence is golden flows the brook
Where local boys with straw in their gobs
Are gathered round a pond
Kick at the moon's reflection and grunt
But still there is no sound

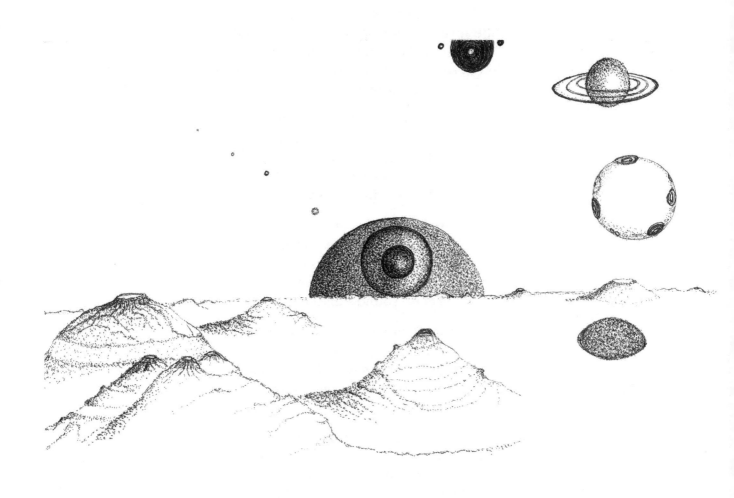

There is a Poulshot red with
The setting sun where a
Raven sits but now just knits his toes
He used to croak but his voice has broke
Where once raucous crows
Fall silent as snow
Tread softly on the soil
And everywhere
People stare silent
As they toil

A fee is bought my some odd sorts
And the stream gushes forth to a pound
So we pull from that tree setting it free
From a creeper like snake round its girth
And the crazed man smiles his thoughts beguile
Shaking from head to foot with mirth

And a thousand ivy strands
Are wrought to a rope
And up it we climb and climb
Proudly step out on Orion's belt
His dagger now I have found
I am the hunter I am the hunter
As far as my eyes can see
And my voice is heard from down below
As they dance in a revelry

BOXING DAY 2016

So still Boxing day 2016
So quiet and still the sheep unseeing look about
Something prowling silently by their keep
Those storms have passed around
Too shy to make a sound
In case someone heard and wondered why

So calm and yet the pins in the haystack
Dropped
Make no noise until they're found
The muted kettles barely whistle
As homeward smile the shepherds
Under a bleeding sky

In the needle's eye
A two humped camel slips
Through on the sly
In the farm yard hardly a word
The dogs whimper in their sleep
Shhhh! the cows do creep
Where the milkmaid trips and
Slides on the cobbled pladdy

A butterbreath Angel heaves her buxom chest
Lifts her brimming buckets as she sighs
Looking west
Another year gone the setting sun
Her chastity
Unblessed

CIGARETTE SEQUEL

...Misted up window's evaporated centre
Revealed the river outside the glass
The place was condensed in every sense
The drink the smoke the breathing mass
It seemed to hold the place together
Like some impenetrable impasse
This room, huge breathing smoking lung
This saloon bar - drink damp and wrung
The carpet stuck the souls of feet
"Are you gonna listen to this?" my entreat
"Yeah sure!" she giggled got comfortable
Wriggled chin in hands, fell still

Do I have the pill I thought I wrestled and I fought
This is the girl who blew smoke in my eyes
God knows what she thought then I steadied
And I let the poem out at will

"Of Fish!"

Him the fish
She the water
Gregarious as he shoals
The flashing sides of fish canter
Through her invisible soul

White sided gazelles reflecting
Slicing blades on flanks collecting
Silvery shanks of shell-emblazoned
Lubed by her liquid veins
Driving the fish insane

120

Scales quiver gills are gasping
Before the explosive quake
Will they make it out of her slippery grasp
Up the waterfalls rasping face?"

"Give up!" she interjected slid out of her moistened seat
Jumped to her feet
" I need some bloody breath!"
Drew a cigarette and smoked it down to the filters end
"Slow down!" she panted moving closer ready for the kill
"Break it up too much info... its driving me round the bend!"

The rivers roar shut out the surface
Like a door
Between the air and him crashed
Over the wall and through the window
Drenching the pub within
He was reaching over to catch her lips
When the firemen rushed in...

Is it all too thin too thin too thin...
Is it all to thin too thin

CROOKIE

I hear in the cuckoo return
Life ebbing as a long lost friend
Time burns
Images gone
Newspaper prints
Yellow in the sun

That enigmatic call which
Winds like a creeper along
Fence and rotting rails
Dilapidated hang
Broken gates
Left open
Spirits long bolted

Begun

It relates
Sonorous its oboe call
From Folly oaks
Across to Potternewick vale

Where woods perish
Revealing worn out words
Teeth crenulated in rusted
Nails

Sombre yet fresh it coils

And in that wakening dawn refrain
I hear the rush of the thrush
Declare his name

Repeating again and again
Crookie Crookie Crookie

Across the shires out to the
Sun and moon

Catching the tails of retreating stars
And its bouncing echoes
From Mercury to Mars

On and on as it filters back
Down
Falls
His largesse recalls and
Soon rests to coalesce in my
Consciousness

THE WATER VOLE

Long gone now old ratty
From these local water's shores
The like we'll never see again
And never seen before.
On the road to man-delay
All those dreams from olden days
The bittern too I never saw and sadly
They that ought to gladly have done
All are blown away

I remember old boys in the pubs
As they rubbed their baccy say
How every hay field cut was smitten
By the booming cry of bittern
But my first cigarette card-
I was young and learnt hard
'Wildlife in Britain' my favourite two
Was of a water vole and that extinct bird so
Through hippocampus function
Of that organ in the brain
Sat at the mouth in a shadowy grain
A photograph of the old canal
Where I played with my young school pals
A soft brown memory down a drain
Rotten lock gates slowly swaying
Gently groaning in the rain

You asked me if I heard the steam train
If I'd seen the moon and the sunset wane
And the opening locks and the gold licked flocks
Of wood quest rock dove stock doves
And rooks dispersed from cut corn fields
To coo and to cackle in high treetops
The creak and groan of the opening gate unlocked
The water came in with a gush to the pound
As down the lane the fishermen laughing boasting
Push their tackle homeward bound

Out it came...when all was clear out of its hole
The water vole appears then in it plopped
Furiously paddling through chick weed strands
Avoiding coots and moorhens on lily stands
And the hiss of swans as they sail by
Seriously addled revellers oars
As they poured themselves out of boats
As bats flew low I remember now
We sat entranced and watched the show
The water rat dived when it heard the owl hoots
Hauling itself out and licking its coat
Beady eyes aware of predatory stoats

125

And also I remember as the memory lasts
The water vole and its repast chewing on a long stem
Till all was gone and starting on another of them
Frenetically
Swimming like a clockwork chuff chuff train
A living sculpture kinetically
Back and forth again and again from bank to bank
Sampling herbs and slender reeds of ranunculus flanks
Ignoring swans that stabbed at bread as it sank
As it swam swam swam across a lock pound dam
And it seldom heard the wind through the willows
Frankie Howerd and Googie Withers
Sleeping sound on a bed of mossy pillows
Up with the lark on a sedge raft to sit on
And remembering as it breakfasted
The long gone bittern

DELPHINUS CIRCUMPOLAR WEND

I strolled down long avenues
Of glass topped cabinets of bones
In the distance humming 'puters
Chill call of telephones
Down aisle 'pon aisles exhibits lay
Along corridors empty of a single life
My feet slapped up to the remains
A prostrate marine mammal and his wife

Where is Delphinus then
Shout the two stargazers
Out the door and staring up
We saw it in the summer called
Mimi and Will from the window sill
It disappeared when the rain set in
Where does it end
Where does it begin
The antonym the synonym
We haven't seen it any more
So we gave up again

...Above me as if a sign to say
I glimpsed her in a spray of light
A million trillion light years sail
From the enigmatic Milky Way
As clouds broke a silver seal revealed
A dream broke in my head
A dolphin saved a poet strayed
It saved him drowning mystics said
As I too fall from out my metaphoric boat

Cry similes of prayer and hope

I took this constellation then
And watched it circumpolar wend
From late summer best it
Lends a view
To darkest winter northern hangs
Near Vulpecula fox's lair
With opened fangs it bares
Sagitta and Aquila just stare
While Equuleus and Pegasus glare
Smote their hooves streaming manes
Exploding stardust everywhere
Some narrative which I've construed
Delphinus sparkles there again

Oooh! how cruel the north wind blew
In words of snow from me to you
And from a Christmas song it grew
And flakes fell as music notes
Descending to a frozen earth
In lace sewn parachutes

A white stew swirled the world
Inside a shaker figures skated
Streams and rivers in a stasis
Sending shivers as they quivered
Their ice cracked waters
Concuss fish suspended
There in aspic dishes

Inside the engine of these veins
Pulses quaked and tremors triggered
White arteries burst thrombotic fissures
A dolphin burst a cataract
And in that joy-momentous act all
Energy released into the sea
Calls of seagulls on the ropes
Thawed frozen through to their poles
That sentient mammal gives such hope
To drowning souls like
Me an' you

And from the earth there came a sound
Which emanated from the ground
A sort of groan which grew to be
A loud and resonant lament
Plangent interstellarly
A resolute testament tantamount to
Winding through the fundament
Like plucked upon a harpsichord
Morphed into a chanted word

Delphinus Delphinus Delphinus!

Staring up I caught it lying
As snow clouds scud across the sky
I stared and stared and stared to see
If formed a word of dolphin glee
Would come a phrase of comforting

Yet from all that frozen light
Nothing freed me from my plight
Still 'long as it is visible
That mammal's surely biddable
So yet in hope I write and write
And write and write...
Till Delphinus fades again
Out of sight...

YEW TREES AT GLOAMING HOUR

Red eyes embedded
Staring out swollen lidded
Pinpointed pupils glare

And from within as
Emerald shadows fall
No darker margins hold
Such rubies galore
A form hides unseen
Camouflaged in green

The volume turned down
On robin's repertoire
Before the owl
Silhouettes all noises
Soon inside the hour ...

And only when the malachite
Caused by yew and sky to blend
There springs a nest of
Gold spun light suspended
Which emanates from a cluster
Of far flung stars
Into which the berry sits
On its transitory brief
As interloping Mars

ALL IN A NIGHT'S DREAM

A silver repoussé she-wee piss pot
For womens' undeclared aborted flights white whale's pink
Gelatinous eye embedded in it's
Bacon form mouths silently from behind
The antique warped glass shop window swims out
The door ajar into the dull decaying Paris-
Ian air cat's eye along a wet run-
Wayed road be down and stroke it's purring weep-
Ing nose and at the tip of yonder slim slen-
Der prehensile limbs gripped in a vice un-
Able to withstand a tremor as the
Organ grows bursts into an opened palm

The psalm an exploded crescendoed ten-
Der petalled rose falls on the metalled road
Silverware that's been hitten out by a
Hammer's blow never grows back unlike the
Petals of a smitten rose reform... grow

131

INSIDE OUT I SPUN

As I woke up one morn so frail
Above Crookwood brook I sailed
I raced its rills and bends and spills
And found its source
From Urchfont to
Worton coursed
And as the wind rushed in my face
Clouds of lace raced
Up above now were stars inside out like paper shards
And on each a message I could read
A language like some creed
An isthmus to another breed
Ahead of me a presence grew
Into a body massively

Crescent moons and popping suns
Across a rainbow were born
And all set out around me slung
Round planets half spun
As in a bed of hope I swung
And gripped so tightly
I clung
The ropes undone
My mooring gone
Untethered a
Dawn sail begun

Suddenly a fog horn voice exploded
I don't know much more than you
But what I do know's rarely viewed
Follow me and you will be
Everything you want to see

I can't I can't I can't hold on
Something you said I'd done
I wanted to explain...
Then inside out I spun
Across a rainbow

THE WHITE TRIANGLE

...and upon his proud chest emblazoned
Crest a white triangle
As if it held significance it shone
And through grey limbs sprung along
Carried boughs of sturdy green heart oak
Was carried into fray...
His sombre face is no disgrace
As if atrophy itself is wasting away
His giant footprints in greensand
Imprinted hieroglyphs of power
Where e'er he lands
And in the shouts of sound
He suffers clowns for

He has already found there's nothing more frightening
Or dangerous than
A frightened man

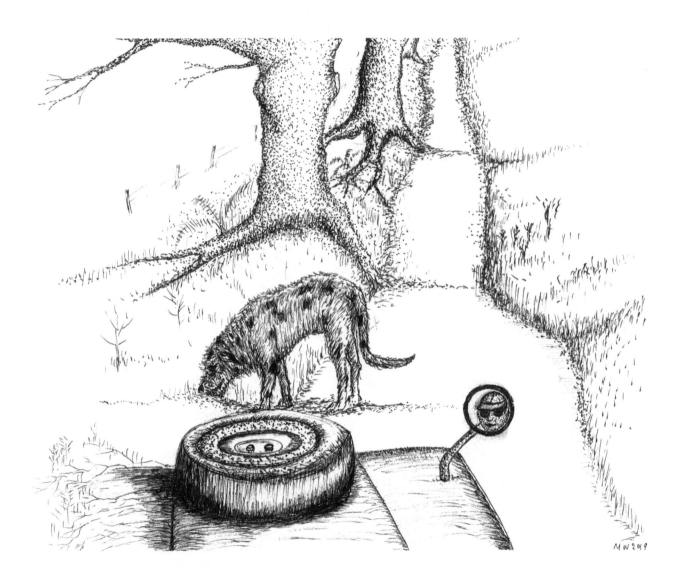

THE WORT

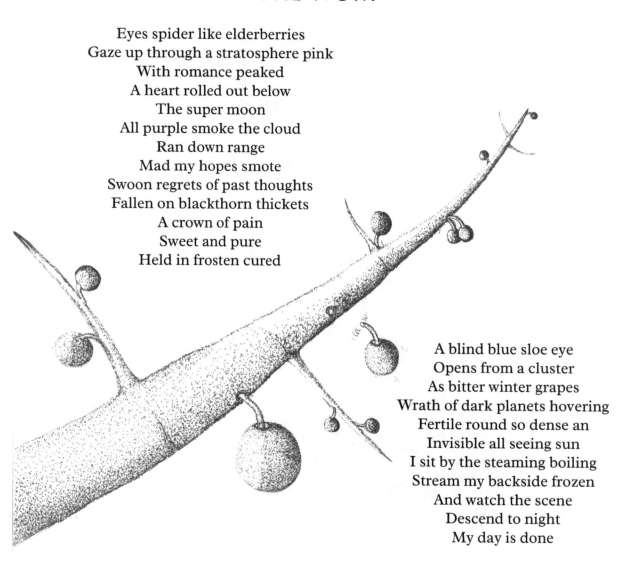

Eyes spider like elderberries
Gaze up through a stratosphere pink
With romance peaked
A heart rolled out below
The super moon
All purple smoke the cloud
Ran down range
Mad my hopes smote
Swoon regrets of past thoughts
Fallen on blackthorn thickets
A crown of pain
Sweet and pure
Held in frosten cured

A blind blue sloe eye
Opens from a cluster
As bitter winter grapes
Wrath of dark planets hovering
Fertile round so dense an
Invisible all seeing sun
I sit by the steaming boiling
Stream my backside frozen
And watch the scene
Descend to night
My day is done

DON'T CRY

Day fades slowly, shadows deepen
Dim twilight shades a dusky world
Mists merge, drift and shroud the evening
Now pitter-patter sounds of rain
Surge to a more collective drone
Soak'd trees huddle in the downpour
Darkness advances, embracing
The lakes fringes and the waters edge
One no longer sees the shape nor form
The night sky and the stars have gone
Always the rain comes on and on
This is a wet and lonely place
We lie here, part of the cold earth
We are the night waiting for dawn
Hey don't listen to me
About keeping love
I can't catch a cold
And keep it -sweet thing
You fell from the sky
I don't know why

I don't know why
You couldn't fly
Something shot through you
While in the sky
Don't die don't die soft bird
I'll try and try
I aunt as brave as you you know
So light as a feathered angel

If I was to fly I'd
Protect me by an armoured suit
Of thickened hide so heavy inside
And that's maybe why
I cannot fly

And I can't tell you about love
And compromise
And to possess it
Is to pass it by
You can't buy it little butterfly
And to own it is to live a lie
It's as free
As the birds and all that fly

DUMB STRUCK

Sun blasting off the surface of the Wylie
Ripples like a Grayling's flank
This is where I dropped the bate in
Deep into the jaws - tigers waiting
Doesn't get much better than this
Being frank having a piss where the flies emerge
And spin
When you're feeling sad
This must rank with all the best days I've ever had
Like fishing with my old dad
And racing up the shallows with a Pikey

God her bare cheeks in my face
Struck dumb and unaware
I would never see such beauty again there
In front of me
So brazen
And the haze on the lip of the bend
She turns and curses me again
Disappearing letters send
Cannot spell the words I need

And round and round and round I sin
In the water spill in in above my shins I go
Like some tackle on the end of my shiney
Liney all the
While the windey wiley Wylie
Bends away a silver freckled spine
She flows away
She goes
Without saying
Goodbye
E

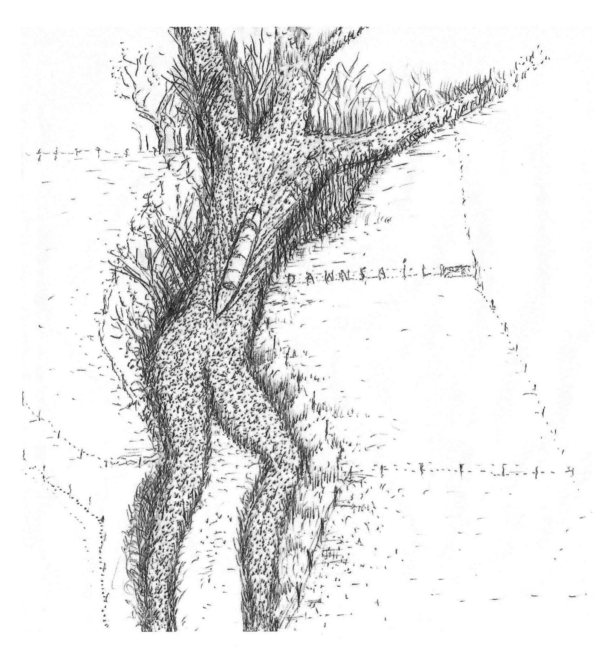

ENTIRE LIKE

This is like the ghost of me now
Wrestled from some low slung slumber
Trying to put my mouth around some word
Placing my tongue in some cleft
And failing
Still grasping but holding little but air

Some people call it freedom
A spirit free from ties and complexities
But I have lived like this my entire life
Answer only to myself
Rarely have I kept relationships
Never have I kept a wife.
I am free yet lonely

The stars purred in the heavens
Fled next a dusty nebula bled
And down to earth light as a feather
I twist and spiral floating
Land upon an old farm trailer
By a babbling brook
An old sheep shakes its fleece and looks

I never cried much when I was young
For beauty born out of the sun
Of all those fantastic aspirations
Of such things undone
So busy shouting idealistic flings slings begun
All half done
I sinned and threw caution to the wind
I did the opposite of everything I was told

But now as time has run its courses
And I am old
I am of course more contemplative
Of my limitations and resources
Running out

I sit here on this careworn chassis happy
By this stream and dream and wonder
Why I never did team up with anyone
For long
I crack a few walnuts but no chimes or gong
Tell me when the day is half gone or done
On this old threshing wagon I repaired
I can be heard humming the songs which haunt
My soul of hearts I stole

I have parked it under a mighty oak tree
Its cavernous shade like some cathedral vault
Echo birdsong like sweet woodbine curling down
Where I dream and dream and dream
Steaming in the morning mists
And silently remember how in those distant
Septembers seem my birthdays glowed
And sparked like kicked embers in a fire

Leaves turned from green to brown
Lithe limbs desire from summer
Gold entwined
When I was sold on love...

And once not so long ago
So late I lingered
I'd fallen asleep
As I fingered through some words
I had so often reread
But usually when I was home curled up in bed
And not prostrate on an old wagon instead
Open to the night and all it held
Flittering bats squeaked and swerved
Past owls welded to their perch
Eerily orchestrated badgers grunting
While searching prey
Through the hedge bore holes
Where rabbits played

A hunting fox slunk by and barked
A vixen lonely as me
I sat up with a jolt
And blew on my cold hands
And from them cupped
Some magic did erupt

The red fox threw back her head
In a trance like state
My mouth so dry I licked my trembling lips
She raised her red eyes
Up at the blood red moon
Red too I sat in that eclipse
So empty her heart did smart and burn
She howled and ran

And I ran with her into the purple blackness
As if entire-like
And till you read this piece
I never did return

EPIPHANY

I went and sat beside a tarn
As the moon slipped low beneath a cloud
My heart was beating
So loud
From that long somnambulant walk from my restless bed
And underneath a laced shroud
My thoughts spoke as if they sat beside me there now

Where below me in the distance cowed
The sleeping village woke some how
And glowed

In a whisper something stirred
And with strange words
I understood because the voice was part of me
Yet it was of things I had not felt before

An epiphany woke as dawn broke
And something in the waters edge hidden in the margin sedge
Floated wedged by lied a rock

As birdsong grew I heard through it a female troubled voice crying a volley of sad words
Reach out to grab me like from a passing ghost
Which made the hairs arise upon my form
Then silence which lent gravity as I fell back behind me
Into the vacuum
Left by my empty self

I sat upon a frozen plate and thawed
A frosted sparkle satellite
Left its driven furrowed path in space and circled overhead
Reflecting in my pallid face

It was me lying as the waters lapped and from the orbit light was said
We will come again
To this place of yoúrs

In a dream I drowned
But before too late I came around and swallowed plenty of the lake
And recovered coughing in my shallow bed
Rolling over in my throbbing head
The things played out and vowed to myself
To return again and again
To that waters edge...

145

EXTRAPOLATE

...my dreams produce fantastic themes
and in them time suspends and seems
to walk away with me...

That idea crawling across tectonic plates
Strata red rock cracks to make
An outline of a vertebrae
And from a crouched position
Wakes a dragon
Rises and surveys

It takes one step and then another
Is it my Jurassic brother
He has found
Light-years hence upon this ground
I double take and hear a sound
A roar from distant times before
Who looked out like me across this place
And stares deep down into my face

And down his throat I slide and tumble
While echoes out amongst the jungle
My ape-like breast beats
A rumble

So from all my dreams and follies
I am transported off my trolley
Caged inside guerrilla form
Striding through the flora fauna

Roaring at the lightening storms
And blinking thoughtful even
And when I'm calm
Staring out and sat alone
Across this Eden vale below
I call my kingdom home
Chewing on a finger nail
Contemplating

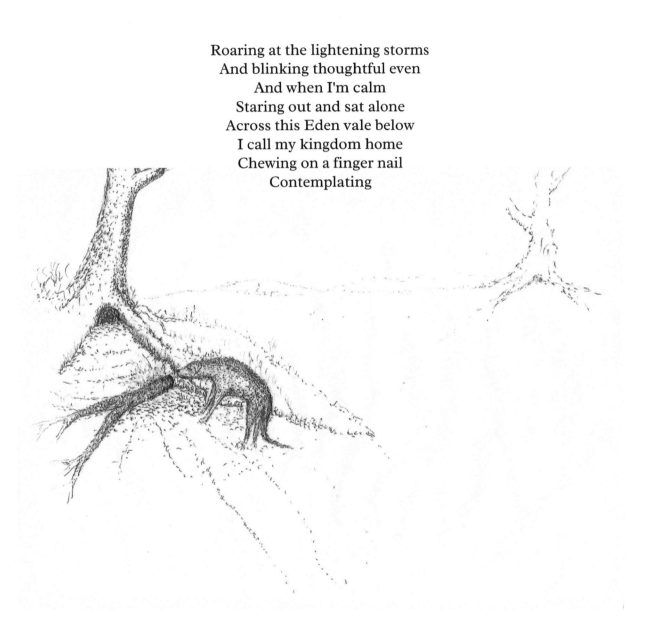

GLIDE

There is a purpurite shade
Shadowing my heart
Descends
A green band encircling
Your wrist and hand
Reaches up
Of delicate unopened flowers
And tressles of your hair

Where is the sentiment now lost
Only the merest wisp of scent
Caught in a gasp of frost
In blasts of coldening air
Between your lips
My friend

And on the window pain
Inside my gloom
Droplets of water condensed
From my heated breath...
Cause blurred undeciphered
Hieroglyphics
As they melt

Outside myself my lungs exhale
And winter rushes into my soul place
It chases me down a throated strictured
Fellow paen tube
Into the opening of an enlarged
Igloo womb

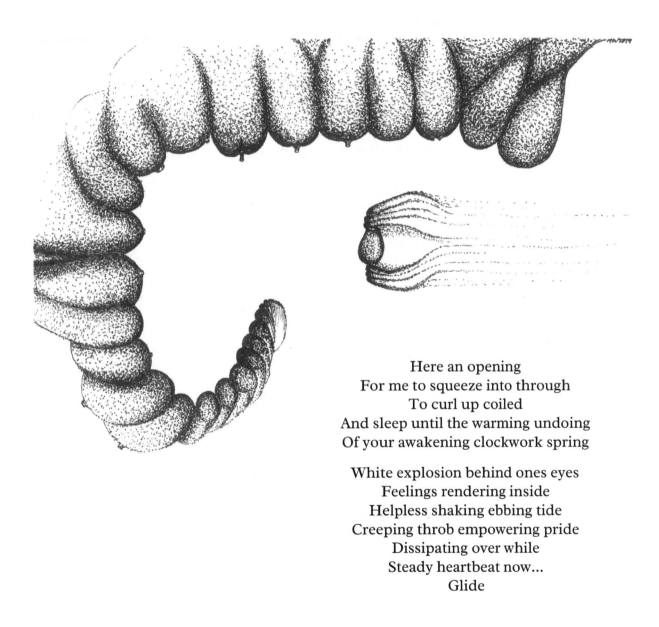

Here an opening
For me to squeeze into through
To curl up coiled
And sleep until the warming undoing
Of your awakening clockwork spring

White explosion behind ones eyes
Feelings rendering inside
Helpless shaking ebbing tide
Creeping throb empowering pride
Dissipating over while
Steady heartbeat now...
Glide

149

THE LONG DISTANCE

Maybe some day I will go back
have travelled enough to see the world
Will always return to some place I remember
For I have travelled almost everywhere

And in those days savoured
Should we view the place secondary
For it is constant
Surely the people there recalled
We should cherish most
Yet people are everywhere
But sometimes those precious people
Go off around the world
As we chew on our fat
Unaware
Some pass away and
Are not forever here or there

One person lasts
In the dark recesses of my distant past
Only one person I would like to see
If only to try and set them free
For years my conscience has troubled me
For I had left her all at sea

To come upon her in those woods
The full moon setting alight her pallid face
Or in her lonely room one night
While she still prays there to a candle
For my soul's sake
Ignorant only of what my destiny or fate

She knows me inside out
And more
Than even I know of myself
For she endured the time
I have left her on
An unrequited shelf

...I wish I could knock lightly
On your half opened door
Step softly to your
Warm inviting bed
Kiss you gently
On your silent lips
An quietly leave forever

Your hand barely holding
A crumpled tissue
Your saintly brow
Relaxed from issue
Just sleep suspended
You in form
Before the day's
Idea dawns

But I have hundreds
Miles to ponder
The never ending
Road out yonder
And grinding mindless thoughts
To keep me
From falling
At this wheel
Asleep

TWO GREAT LADIES

Sun's dappled tiling
Decorate high green sand walls
Shaking like chandelier reflections
As the breeze calls
Through the fluted columned
Fan vaulted trees
Pigeons like oboe notes
Fall from above in azure blue
Gently down a scale bursting
A canopied double aspect
Rose window
When where through
Colours explode and scatter
On a cool dusty floor

Two great ladies embark
Upon the Folly track
Great not in stature but
In every thing I lack
Each asking questions of
Osteoarthritic backs

Pigeons flap away startled
Applauding in their clap
I gaze at my sketch of them
Caught with one snap
A second in time
From a dripping tortured tap
Onward they slowly climb

They don't look back

Unaware of all about them
'Cept of which they talk about

Against great historic upheavaled tides
Waves they have swum
And saved and saved
To enable we to succeed
Decades of self deprivation
Their seeds they gave
Unconditional maternal love
Their now threadbare tattered emblems
Still rippling atop their lances
Masts stand firm unfurled flags
Of hard fought stances...
Peace

Please do come
And sit and ease those aching boughs
Yet... stepping out those tough old boots
Once supple -squeak

Holding hands
To counter gravity
All through- life's problems solved
Hanging onto it with steel
Like resolve
Sibling regard
Steps softly
Up the hill and back
They stoop pick and blow together a
Dandelion seeded colonel

...Encapsulates a love-
Enduring pact...
Eternal

COMING SOON

SAILING WITH
O' FAOILEACHA'IN